THE HAT
AND
OTHER
POEMS
AND
PROSE

IVAN KLEIN

Also by Ivan Klein

Grateful acknowledgment is made to the editors of the following journals in which some of these pieces originally appeared: *Urban Graffiti,* the *Jewish Literary Journal, The Forward, Arteidolia, Swifts and Slows, Otoliths, Flying Fish,* and *Poetry Super Highway.*

Published by Sixth Floor Press, New York, NY

SIXTH FLOOR PRESS

info@sixthfloorpress.com

Cover painting (untitled) by Koho Yamamoto, photographed by Phyllis Klein. Reprinted with permission.

ISBN 978-0-578-85730-5

Thanks as always to my wife Phyllis for her help with this manuscript, and to my son David, the MVP of this volume.

For Asher

Contents

Meditation on
Gao Xingjian's <u>Soul Mountain</u>

Is there a way to this so-called Soul Mountain of his?
And why are we wandering this cluttered earth if not to find it?

Through the underbrush & rocks & deep gorges & running
rivers going nowhere;
past misleading directions of provincial persons and small-
minded officials—
past all the talk & futility of unfocused sex & unrealized
feelings, on to the highest ground of the experience of pure being—
Is there such a way
to such a place?
And why would we be wandering this cluttered earth
if not to find it?
He hears a flitting rumor of an ancient text with directions to
the next world that will take us there & to some place called home at
the same time. A better place than the common dust we come from is
the elusive promise...and I ask myself what I'm looking for & how I'm
killing time in this exile I call my life & hope this search is for real & that
all other bets are off...
On the path to Soul Mountain there are common grey snakes
with dull eyes that strike like lightning to absolutely sudden deadly
effect.
There are interminable humdrum yin/yang conversations

with a girl whose heart and cunt are elsewhere;

And demon shadows dancing our own dance, mimicking our affrighted selves, scaring us out of our wits as we shine our lanterns into the black mountain night.

A peasant tells the seeker that humans can't overcome fate & he wonders, "If my soul showed itself, could I understand it?" — And what would be the consequences if it really exists and if we really could?

The final message of the venerable Buddhist master of Soul Mountain long ago was   pure paradox understood by no one, not even his closest disciples.

— Someone who he loves who loves him, is that what it boils down to? — after all the Buddhists, Taoists, magicians, shamans—more elusive than the Holy Grail, more elusive, finally, than all the wisdom the universe could possibly proffer.

Look hard enough in the mist on Soul Mountain
And see a lost city of incontinent would-be Buddhas turned to ashes and dust;

Then see nothing at all.

Also, is it true then that the dragon of creativity is no match for the snake of malice?

———————

The longing for the perfect mate, — a graceful dancer with silver anklets tinkling with little bells, a red mouth, perfect little feet, teeth like sparkling pearls—and then there is the wind in the cave on the mountain, brutal, blowing through the hole in your old heart.

Is the cave on the mountain a dream?
The dancing girl you heard & saw a dream?
Perhaps it is death & old age you are dreaming.
Humdrum yin/yang conversations with ordinary girls:

an ordinary man simply killing time.
Dream or reality so-to-speak,
it's all the same to us,
to him and me.
But no, don't die like this, in the mists of a mountain that
doesn't exist,
Back stage in a nightmare that won't go away;
far, far from the world of real human beings,
from the decent possibility of love.
No, not like this.

———————————

The woman tells him that she loathes him, that he is going straight down to the King of Hell from this so-called Soul Mountain;

that she is going back to her old man, no matter that he knocked her around a bit & talked about other women when they fucked; now she realizes that he loved her & only talked about other cunts when they made love in order to turn her on...

Not like you, you creep...who abuses my mind with myth & metaphysics

He winds up talking to his shadow on the winding mountain road & thinks himself better off...dreams & desires all jumbled up...

He's searching for his childhood memories among other things while I'm running away from mine, feigning amnesia—they come & go as they please in my empty defenseless mind. It's all too shameful, too frightened, too small & difficult. I'd rather simply wrestle with death & the demons of hell than the awful sea of recollection...

He comes down from Soul Mountain, no haircut in months, looking like a wildman, a writer now somewhat famous, reading the palms of hordes of pretty girls, reading them in a most cunning & penetrating manner, claiming shamanistic powers.

———————————

Proud

stupid

alone

getting ready to die.

No friends to speak of, an afterthought to my children. All my plans come to naught—it doesn't seem so bad when I look at it in a certain light...

The first book born within us:

To articulate that book is the great task of a writer's life—

The mystery of this elusive and primary book, of cellular truth greater than mere autobiography or personal mythologizing.

—What do our lives say when they speak truly to us, in what language do these lives speak & how can we translate them into the general tongue?

The author of Soul Mountain searches out pre-Confucian folk songs...

Give me the day, the month, the year song was born, give me the principle of heaven & earth; give me back myself from this meaningless chaos.

"With Yin there is language,

With Yang there is sound."

Somehow man finds himself born & hears himself singing in pain & wonder. – In the dark he hears the beating of a drum and is no longer alone.

Soul Mountain

The Record of Darkness

The ancient death songs of the primordial Han people suppressed and destroyed by the bureaucracy—

"A race with empty, desolate souls!" the author exclaims. He believes the age of poetry is over; that everything has already been sung or rhythmically shouted—everything worth singing or shouting all said and done.

—just impressions left—somewhat vague inkblots, I suppose.

He beats it quickly from the Taoist Temple Of Supreme Purity—he's too attached to himself, to his heart, to that cute little trick in the guise of a Taoist nun. He's not really interested in anyone else's suffering, in the persecution stories of the old Taoist priests, how they managed to save a remnant of their holy books from burning at the hands of the authorities. No, he can't be bothered with anyone else's suffering; he is himself & nothing makes more sense than that. And his precious heart, he wishes to preserve it, just for himself alone.

> [for his own use—from the forces of destruction which are everywhere and include practically everybody and everything]

He also tells us that he recoils from both beauty and evil...tells us that his probable (hypothetical) tragedy is needing a normal life.

Deep down in the dark forest of dead trees with its living, disapproving eyes, he runs screaming toward the valley of forgetting—women companions, crying children abandoned in the dust of the traveler's road for the urgent needs of what we'll call his living spirit.

Looking at a blank mirror in an abandoned temple, he sees only an empty blue sky.

Having been to the mountain, he is still asking directions and trying to find his way there—The wind howls; a solitary man is blown about; a frog blinks; a soul ascends or descends to no place at all that allows itself to be known.

Before Michelangelo's Moses

Unlike Hannibal who fatally hesitated and never quite made it through the gates of Rome, Freud gets there in his 45th year, surmounting formidable psychic roadblocks to do so.

He visits the basilica of San Pietro in Vincoli, beholds the horned, seated statue of Moses, finds it wonderfully compelling and returns each summer on what become annual pilgrimages to the Eternal City. Thirteen years after his first encounter, he publishes an anonymous piece in the magazine "Imago", which explores the strong feelings the sculpture evokes in him. He finds it "inscrutable" and "wonderful" and gives us this extraordinary passage:

"How often have I mounted the steep steps from the unlovely Corso Cavour to the lonely piazza where the deserted church stands, and have essayed to support the angry scorn of the hero's glance! Sometimes I have crept cautiously out of the half-gloom of the interior as though I myself belonged to the mob which can hold fast to no conviction, which has neither faith nor patience, and which rejoices when it has regained its illusory idols."

He's busted by the horned figure's power, by its look of absolute contempt for the slavish rabble beneath him.

This seated Moses, haughty and disdainful, presses the tablets of the law against his right side – these rough slabs are mine – the word is mine – you are loathsome to me and the God that I gave you!

The fingers of the right hand are embedded in the magnificently executed marble beard; the left hand is way low down on his abdomen, gripping the end of its flowing serpentine mass. – Simultaneously holding on to its god law and the excrescence of his all-powerful manhood.

> The wrath of the self-righteous,
>   self-absorbed father
> of which nature has no equal.

Vengeance is his to dispense. – Freud felt this right off – that vengeance was his first instinct. As if Moses was the omnipotent and jealous God of the Hebrews rather than his interlocutor.

He feels himself guilty as charged for being part of
    the orgiastic mob,
For giving himself outright to the glistering young bull;
Guilty for being just another bloodthirsty member of that very nearly primal hoard
    he will later refer to as the savage Hebrews of the Sinai desert;
Guilty with them of terminal disobedience and the offing of

the punitive and restrictive father, Moses, in some obscure byway of
the dark past.

(This according to his own theory of the thing.)

Not-so-proud possessor of the pure Jew guilt laid upon us for
the murder
of God, Father and Son.

A guilt to which he finds that we alone of all the peoples,
with unfathomable obstinacy,
Will not cop a plea, thus making our suffering and the rage against us
a hundred times worse.

Horns

In the <u>Moses and Monotheism</u> of his last exilic years, he
professed to be "astonished to learn that there are [those] who find
nothing to admire in the Moses but who revolt against it and
complain of the brutality of the figure and the animal cast of the
head."

I stand with those who astonish him, who can't abide its epic
contempt, its finally ludicrous and mistaken goat horns tilted slightly
forward.

> This daunting horned figure,
> A marbled imposture
> Like unto the gods of the Greeks,

> To whom we did not knuckle under,
> Before whom we make no apologies for living.

———————————

Habakkak 3:3-4

> It is a brilliant light
> which gives off rays on every side —
> And therein His glory is enveloped.

A radiance like a reflection from off the sun emanates from Moses as he descends smoldering Mount Sinai after his second and decisive encounter with the Lord.

A radiance that overwhelmed the Hebrews waiting down below in darkness and led Moses to veil himself when he walked among them.

This effulgence rendered in the Vulgate by Jerome as Moses being "horned." – What the <u>Oxford Jewish Study Bible</u> politely suggests to be an "overly etymological translation."

Heb.: "Karan" – radiance <— from "Keren" – horn.

Moses with horns conflates with the horned Satan and the world's belief that the Jews as members of the Devil's party have horns as well. – So that we are left with the certain knowledge that things have never really been on the up and up. – So that every possible suspicion fell upon us, every catastrophe came home to us.

Michelangelo horns his Moses over a thousand years after Jerome, and the horned belief persists to this day, dwelling subtly and not so subtly at the very heart of things.

Curiously, Freud finds Michelangelo's sculpture, commissioned for the tomb of "the warrior pope" Julius II, morally and emotionally superior to the biblical prophet; he sees this Moses as captured in the act of suppressing his passions, avoiding the shattering of the tablets, "for the cause to which he has devoted himself." — The art object as a lesson in constraint to everyone concerned, including the artist.

In that limitation, in the historical revision which Freud perceives as flowing from the figure's posture, perhaps he finds an emotional amnesty for himself and his unruly tribe.

Still, he can't look it square
    in the eye,
Slouches away from the basilica
            like a thrice cursed Jew man.

Busted and played,
            crushed by the weight
                of history,

By the judgment he has tendered
    against himself and his father
            before him.

The Hat

Freud, in his mid-thirties, is traveling through Italy, partially following in the footsteps of his boyhood hero, the great Carthaginian general, Hannibal, when a series of associations lead him to the recovery of the repressed childhood memory of a story told to him by his father, Jakob.

He writes that when he was ten or twelve years old, Jakob began to take him along on his walks "and his conversations to reveal his views on the things of the world." He tells him of a particular incident with the avowed purpose of showing the boy "that he had been born in happier times" than his father:

As a young man in the small Moravian village in which Sigmund was later born, Jakob was walking along the street all dressed up with a new fur hat on his head when a Christian came along and knocked it into the mud of the road and said, "Jew, get off the pavement!"

"And what did you do?" was the naked question of the son.

"I went into the roadway and picked up my cap," the father quietly replied, and Freud notes that this struck him as "unheroic conduct on the part of the big strong man holding the little boy by the hand."

This devastating found memory would remain in Freud's dreams and waking consciousness thereafter.

One imagines the father warmly holding on to his young son, feeling him as a formative projection of his own self and speaking (perhaps for the very first time) of that awful humiliation of his young manhood. But the ostensible reason for the telling – the use of the incident to illustrate the progress that the Jews had made over the course of a generation – is at least as distressing as the raw content of the story itself.

Was Jakob really so oblivious to the effect his account would have on the especially sensitive boy beside him? So blind to the history of his people as to not grasp that his son would be tested as he had been tested and found wanting on that obscure village street? Wasn't he aware in the deepest and truest part of himself of the eternal meaning and peril of the epithet "Jew" as enunciated by his personal emissary from the Christian world?

In <u>The Interpretation of Dreams</u>, Freud contrasted Jakob's craven conduct and the tragic assumptions that shaped his account with the historical scene drawn by Livy in which Hannibal's father, Hamilcar Barca about to go off to war in Spain, swears his nine year old to vengeance against the Romans before the family altar. Between those two existed the generational bonds of Semitic honor that had decayed so terribly over the millennia of Jewish exile. The redoubtable Hannibal would remain a figure of admiration to the founder of psychoanalysis while during his college years when his "dissatisfaction with the conduct" of his father toward the adversaries of their people surfaced, he daydreamed of having a sire such as Hamilcar.

Poor Jakob just scraping by
in the face of the enemy!

It's as if he had told his mortified son
We are Jews here, enlightened
or not;

This is the way it is
and will be.

Grow ghetto walls around
your heart,

Submit and survive.
I tell you this
while at the same time
my soul is overflowing
with love and terror for
you, my son.

The contemporary Israeli critic, Yosef Yerushalmi, addressing Freud as if he were still with us, wrote:

"... I believe you had learned by then [his old age] not to condemn your father for having quietly picked his hat out of the mud."

There doesn't seem to have been any real basis, in fact, for this belief, and, of course, Jakob had been dead for a good many years when this forgiveness was presumed to have occurred.

Did Sigmund forgive him when they were both alive?
Did he truly forgive himself for being Jakob's son?

How do we forgive our fathers their moments of wavering, of cowardice, until we have somehow overcome and forgiven our own dishonored selves?

A Portrait of Bodhidharma

We acquire the portrait of Bodhidharma by our friend and neighbor, the master Japanese brush painter, Koho Yamamoto. A portrait that I admired for years when it hung in her Soho studio.

"The best Bodhidharma I've ever seen," I declared to her at a traditional New Year's Day get together shortly before the studio closed after a thirty-year run. "Quite a compliment," she laughed modestly while calling attention to the Indian cast of the portrait's features.

Found deep in storage and delivered to our door by her faithful student and friend, Jaya, who tells me that it does indeed look a bit Indian and for sure she should know.

My molecular history with the great monk begins in the fall of 1965 in a brick walled basement apartment on Ave. C belonging to a friend from work. The very place where I brew my first cup of tea spiked with an LSD-laced sugar cube. Drink that cup of tea to the bottom for all the world and hold on tight to the battered armchair, hoping to find out that I'm not just dirt inside, but fearing that I am.

By and by, a suffering Christ face appears in every sun-fired brick and there is the experience over a period of some hours of certain enigmatic feelings, as if I'm inside a three-sided puzzle with something that might be called love the only way out.

Unschooled, unrefined, lost in the city and my own psyche, I struggle home to my solitary pad on seriously junked up Forsyth St. just before dawn.

The next day idly browse the old Marboro Bookshop on 8th St. where a purple-colored paperback with the title "Zen Buddhism" catches my eye. By one Christmas Humphries I think it was, the head of the Buddhist Society in London. Could my recollection of the name be correct? A reproduction of a painting of Bodhidharma (awakened one) on the front cover. Something about the distance in his gaze brings back the open-ended puzzle from the night before.

Some several hundred trips to follow over the years and a good deal of reading on the subject along the way, and only an idiot would claim to be any the wiser.

But the basic outline of the Zen origin story seems worth sharing as I look up from my journal at Koho's painting propped against a bookcase prepared for hanging. It's the real thing all right – a bowshot down the empty corridor of time from when this terrible old man, the 28th patriarch in a line of direct transmission that began with Gautama, took it in his head sometime in the 5th century of the common era to sail for southern China and spread the authentic doctrine.

Engages the Emperor Wu in a seminal dialogue. The Emperor, a builder of Buddhist temples and an all-around benefactor of the faith, asks the stone-faced teacher what merit his benevolence will accumulate for him in heaven.

— None whatsoever.

— Then what is the nature of the dharmakaya? (lit. the body of the law)

— A vast emptiness with nothing therein.

— Then, who are you?

— I have no idea.

At which point the story has him putting his sandals on his head and walking north. He is supposed to have found a suitable cave and contemplated its rock surface for nine years until importuned by one Hui-Ko to pacify his mind. Roughly shoved outside, Hui-Ko showed his sincerity by cutting off an arm and presenting it to his hoped-for savior.

Ok, if it's going to be like that, whip out this troubled mind of yours, put it on the table and I'll see what I can do. – Whereupon, Hui-Ko was immediately enlightened and became the second Chinese patriarch in the Chan (Zen) line.

There's a classic painting of this scene by Sesshū Tōyō inscribed 1496, notable for the striking brushwork of the cave's textures, Bodhidharma's dogged wall gaze from under his monk's hood and the anxious aura around Hui-Ko's presentation of his severed arm.

The arrival of Koho's painting takes me away from my current preoccupation with the provenance and metapsychology of the <u>Protocols of the Elders of Zion</u> and what might be called the morphology of Jew hatred.

Agony into dust, finally. Maybe just a bit like the dust of the Topaz concentration camp (woke Japanese term) trod by the young girl Masako Yamamoto who produced this marvelously fresh version of Bodhidharma.

Dust surrounded by barbed wire with an American flag flying overhead. Also captured by Koho (the name bestowed by her distinguished teacher, Professor Obata) in an iconic painting from one of the few remaining survivors of the experience.

She renders Daruma [Jap.] bald, his head sloping at severe angles front and back. In the center of his forehead a single brilliant brushstroke suggesting the light and darkness of this world and the next. Thickets of triangular eyebrows above wall-gazing eyes. A bit of a beard, a few masterful lines that create a sense of substance to the bust as a whole. A mouth cast downward, but in its set and determination, a humanity as well as severity. – For me, what most crucially sets this portrait apart.

I invite the ninety-six-year-old artist upstairs to see the painting newly mounted above my desk, and she says she approves of the home it has found. I tell her I will look after it as best I can and pass it on if I am able to someone who will appreciate it for what it truly is. Understanding between us, I'm pretty sure, what in the matter is mere possession and what is transactionally eternal.

Sakutarō Hagiwara & His Iceland –
5 Poems

Onchi's "Portrait of Sakutarō Hagiwara"

He's not quite squared around, but there's enough of him to see that his face is a veined map of abandonment, dissipation, exquisite longing. – Of too much alcohol, cocaine, morphine to too little effect in killing the pain of a soul forever homeless.

What's the use of these paper scraps,

                    I've now lost everything

he wrote in a piece included in his short lyric masterpiece "The
Iceland". The cast-off husband left to care for two young daughters is
quoted by his translator, Hiroaki Sato, as calling the spirit that
animated the work best summed up in what's contained in the word
"scream."

        But the eyes staring at nothing and everything beyond the
ken of portraiture seem to know in and of themselves that at least the
truth of the heart has been written and will stand.

White-Faced Woman

        Hagiwara is not yet thirty years old when he writes to fellow
poet and confidant, Hakusha Kitahara, of what he describes as nearly
his last day on earth. He had been on a bender, had an awful nervous
reaction afterwards and then has "terrible memories of the lips of a
faintly white-faced woman," who laughed at him after intercourse for
his drunken language and behavior.
        Humiliated, his nerves shot, he smashes his head repeatedly
against a wooden post and thinks he's going mad.
        A question as to whether this is memory or hallucination, or
hallucination based on memory, or a ghostly Oedipal dream of
mother nightmare blanco rejecting her lover-son and coldly tearing
him from the arms of Morpheus.
        —That son who had written that a married woman could
best enjoy sex with her husband when she was aware of her mother-
in-law's "mean, watchful eye peering from behind the sliding paper-
door." – That momma's boy in the mold of the archetypal *poète
maudit,* Baudelaire, of whom Sartre wrote "He had such a violent

horror of himself that we can regard his life as a long series of self-inflicted punishments."

Mystery Trains

Trains deeply affected the soul and imagination of this Japanese poet like the great southern bluesmen to whom he is linked by temperament and the impulses of the heart.

1) "Farewell"

> The train is in the station, snorting, chomping at the bit,
>> ready to rumble, ready
>> "... to cross the border
>> beyond the distant signals and the iron road."
> The helpless passengers submit to its
>> terrifying powers, its rampant enthusiasms.
> A student of Schopenhauer, Hagiwara slingshots that awful

engine of power and will, greater than that which our own poor struggling selves possess; catapults it through black space and time, illuminated only by its cyclopean eye.

> Departures   Separations
>> Breakups

> It tramples hearts and souls in its unappeasable
rush to locate the very stations
> of the unknowable

2) "At A Night Train Window"

> The train is oh so dark,
> The fireflies everywhere,
>> the moonless night impregnable.

> The great terrifying question of his and mankind's
> Futurity grows within him and bursts forth
>> As the engine thunders down the track:

>>> "where, where, is my night train going?"

3) "Returning To My Hometown"

> Like a stray dog stripped of its shadow
>> by the cold-blooded sun
>>> Is the poor wretch bereft
>>>> of life's hometown.

>> "The past links to the valley of desolation
>>> The future faces the shore of despair"

> His will in the world broken, he is conveyed along
the tracks to the wasteland's last stop. All his love's in vain.

> Just like deepest Rob't Johnson indigo. – The train leaves
him in the station, leaves the stranger, the drifter behind. It recedes
from sight. His love's gone, all his love.... He's come from nowhere,
come to nowhere
... It's all, all in vain

Max Ernst —
Kasmin Gallery, Spring 2017

"Big Brother: Teaching Staff For A School Of Murderers", by Max Ernst

Big Brother is all eyes and ears – a vaguely military monument of a bronze cap on his smooth buff head, but no heart whatsoever. Coldly set down on stone, could he possibly believe that his enthronement is the result of overwhelming popular sentiment?

Séraphin the Novice –

Blindfolded and hence eternally sightless, he has an antic tongue jutting out of his mouth that may be described as contending toward the all-knowing. Seated somewhere below his sister seraph and fellow undercover operative, he is the saddest comedown from the highest order of the angels.

Séraphim Cherubin –

Eyes, a head, a platform upon which to rest. –
Dubbed by Ernst, the drollest of artists as "la plus belle" – the most
beautiful.

Her knees rather squeezed together – am I
imagining a state of repression, or is that just for appearance's sake?

Paste-Up

— After Paul Celan's "Conversation In The Mountains":

      Jew Klein meets Jew Gross amid the beauty of nature from which they are chronically veiled.

      The poor saps have nothing to call their own in a place where they won't ever belong.

         Loathe the little Jew!
         Loathe the big Jew!

        Who don't belong,
         Who have nothing,
          Who simply offend!

Pure words green & white,
   flow from the glaciers through
      the center of the mountains.

Pure speech not reckoned for Klein and Gross. — A journey in speech to themselves in the mountains,
   a journey to the unloved dead
      in speech tried & true.

— After Rilke's "Duino Elegies":
   When I had a knife & exhaled,

did the angels tremble?

When I smashed the mirror
    of my vanity,
        did they vanish in thin air?

In the Garden
of the Sanitorium *

The poet as madwoman / the madwoman as poet

There to be protected against the vicious radio messaging of
the Nazi cabal that had hunted her down & penetrated the walls of
her one room refugee apartment in Stockholm with their cunning &
all-knowing antennae & microphones.

Protected from herself, from the image of the recently
captured Eichmann's jackbooted, obscene face, the open wound of
her martyred dead.

She walks alone, guilty in the starlit midnight snow,
clutching the living, stirring buds of the frozen tree branch she has
broken off for her very own.

Eyes wide open, poor heart failing,
she begins to compose the music of
the coming Spring in her beloved high German language.

---

* Inspired by a poem by Nelly Sachs, a Nobel Laureate for Literature in 1966,
in the middle of the decade of her frequent psychiatric hospitalizations.

Primo Levi Departing Auschwitz

The gallows & the giant Christmas tree
          side by side
Near Roll Call Square,

The huts where he had suffered, matured
          & survived, the wasteland of the Buna factory site,

All slid past in the slow motion
          of retrospect, of dream,

As did the memories of the demonic,
          calculated attempt to demolish his manhood,
The foraging for rotten potatoes & turnips
          on the frozen ground,
The myriad shades of the dead
          up in smoke.

          Finally, the steel slave gate with its ironic motto,
               sprung from what he would call the heavy, arrogant,
          funereal wit of the Germans, but now, miraculously,
               seen in reverse:
                    "Arbeit Macht Frei"

Ikkyū & His Skeletons *

"Firebird", by Koho Yamamoto

Ikkyū, aka Crazy Cloud, aka Blind Ass, the much beloved
Zen iconoclast of 15th century Japan, who tore to shreds his certificate
of enlightenment at the very time it was bestowed and hit the road,
knew the high and low of things.

Knew the contempt with which mendicants were doled out
their scraps at the back doors of the wealthy, knew the cold wind that
blew through a lonely hermit's hut in the mountains. – Finally, knew
the pomp of an Abbot's purple robes as well.

---

* Based on Ikkyū's *Skeletons*, trans. by John Stevens, from <u>Wild Ways: Zen
Poems of Ikkyu</u> (White Pine Press, Buffalo, NY)

A drinker, a womanizer and an artist, he tried in his old age
to set the record straight on certain spiritual matters in a lengthy
haibun titled "Skeletons."

It begins with a traditional set-up of the Eternal Quest:
"Filled with disgust and longing to liberate myself from the
realm of continual birth and death, I abandoned home and set off on
a journey."

The wanderer finds himself near a deserted little temple at
the base of a mountain before which is an endless field of graves. Out
of this field a pitiful skeleton arises to hip him to the Essential
Doctrine of Emptiness:
          "All things become naught by returning
                    to their origin."
In an uncanny dream, a second skeleton separates himself
from his crowd to address Ikkyū. He reiterates the Doctrine and the
monk immediately counts him as a friend. – The poor spectral fellow
"saw things clearly, just the way they are."

After dark, the skeleton gang disports itself among the
gravestones
                    while the autumn moonlight dances across the
poet's mortal face.

Under the influence of his new pals, waking and sleeping,
his eyes are wide open. He perceives the basis of philosophy, the
structure of the Buddha's thought, the ten realms of existence, taken
together, truly understood, to be no more than dust.

He further makes the bold claim
that death itself is an illusion.
An additional mirage is the belief that when the body dies,
the soul endures.

"A grave error," says Ikkyū,
not at all inclined to kid the public along.

Then he gets down to serious dharma business:
the Buddha preaching for 50 years and the smile of his follower
Kashyapa at his sermon that consisted of the display of a flower.

The silent transmission of mind between them that is the
bedrock of what is called the Mahayana (Great Vehicle).

With this, Ikkyū declares that he has boiled all the sutras
down to their irreducible essence and that this essence will bestow
bliss.

He has a second thought, thinks better of all that:

"Writing something
to leave behind
Is yet another kind of dream.
When I awake I know that
there will be no one to read it."

You can't blame him for hedging his bets on existence and
non-existence. – On making any kind of wager but on the sure thing
of stone silence.

<u>And yet</u> –

There are the poems to Lady Mori, the blind minstrel, the great love of his last years, who could bring his old prick to life like no other. – The memory of her superlative touch that he must have clung to even as he adeptly let go of all else in the empty universe.

Notan [*]

We perform a small service relating to a senior citizen's adjustment in monthly rent for our dear friend and neighbor, Koho Yamamoto. She shyly rings our doorbell a few days later bearing one of her masterpieces of sumi-e as a gift.

Notan:

        Space / balance / dark and light.

    The untitled painting a pure play of these qualities,

        spontaneous / austere / perfect.

---

[*] From a series on Koho Yamamoto.

Suddenly I feel stupendously rich, privileged, as if all the difficulties of life had been lifted not only from me, but from all memories of me back to the anxious ghetto cradle.

It seems to float lightly upward from the rice paper
at the same time as its tethered
to the utmost surety of vision.

— A companion for the rest of my days on this riven earth.

Sigmar Polke: Eine Winterreise ("A Winter Journey") David Zwirner Gallery, June 2016 (Some Impressions)

Out of the scrambled egg of consciousness, out of the opium
peace pipe in the feathered cap of a seated genie / comes the green
leaf jungle
    of forget-ful-ness,
        comes the brown and silver vision
            of a forgotten thought:
    come the red mosaic Himalayas
        of a splashed idea / comes again that nightmare
        that will not yield its rightful name –
        which makes a mess of its nest ... that obliterates
line / color / form ... but stays alive at the very edge of its god-awful
self

———————

    Smack!
        Life dazzles:
At the top of the mast, semaphores flutter while
thought itself embeds the lightning of the sun.

        A faceless pilgrim on an obscure reindeer pauses
            before a universal scream

----

form or its lack thereof;
           either way comes rain
                    &
     the inner life of a tree that
           grows the blues.
     Hidden in the drip
           A tank / a wiseman / an elephant
                being barbequed
& is that the Wandering Jew I see
     underwater
contemplating the Eiffel Tower?
     The nightmare thickens into the sleep of a skeletal dream ...

The cunt of the world – the explosion of its red fire – it
wanders into the volcanic wilderness and onto the bright untitled
seashore.

     The man in the moon is bug-eyed as a crowd
     telescopes the Beast traveling to its very own meridian.

     He weeps for all of it / all of them as some schmuck with
earlaps & a backpack refuses to hear himself think.

     The globe, the man in the moon, the archetypal schmuck,
           finger painted on blue waves;

     finger painted under a black & blue sky
at the very same moment that some poor jerk got his nose

squashed against a reasonable facsimile of West Africa.

———————————

That moon man of ours knows & is horrified
by what he doesn't see

While the fool sits way up top
A man-made tower, the world his oyster.

The schmuck transformed into the universal artist
paints the almost gone world in stitches.

— In memory S.D.

Palme auf Autostoff (Palm Tree on Fabric), 1969

Koho Yamamoto's
Black Sun Painting

That is, the large, unframed canvas done four years ago
when the *sumi-e* master was ninety-three. Just about old enough, it
seems, to have a consummate idea of what she was doing ...

Sitting in close proximity to its considerable mass, I try to think of an apposite title for its ambiguities: "Dissolution"; "Stove In By A Whale"; "Mutability Via Slow Drip" ...

Slowly bringing myself to focus on that almost palpably quivering gelid black sun with its one good eye squinting on all that is undone below – of the wrecks of the sea, the earth, the low-hanging sky. All of it somehow achieving a terrific unconstrained balance.

The innumerable nuances of the painting's grey and blue tones and those subtly concealed red tints inside bold black strokes that could come from nowhere but her very soul. – What other source could have resulted in such a symphony (or antipode of a symphony) of light and shadow?

Notan – light and shadow:
a nearly chaotic balance tight-roped to the symmetry of life and death.
Qualities and mysteries made triumphantly manifest in this late masterwork.

Satish Gujral:
"Christ in the Desert" (1960)

We enter Joshua Tree National Park at the southern edge of the Mojave Desert near sunset, my son David at the wheel of a rented SUV, my wife and daughter-in-law with us. His idea was to get there just after sunset and catch the stars come out in the clear desert air.

The eponymous trees of the park, graceful and slender with their branches raised in such a way as to remind pioneering Mormons passing through of the great leader of the Hebrews with his arms raised in prayer, or of the signal he gave with his outstretched spear to his men hiding in ambush, ready to take the city of Ai.

Some of these trees, more properly understood as marvelously adaptive cactus plants, vandalized during the 2017 government shutdown when park workers were not on the job. And there, as twilight took its brief hold, I did wonder about the delicate relationship of man with his very self and the world from which he and those plants have arisen.

Traveling deeper in the park, we pass the otherworldly rock and sand formations that have prompted comparisons with the Martian landscape as photographed by NASA. There are roadside displays that discuss the people called the Pima Indians who dwelt there nine thousand years ago in what was then an abundant, watered land. People who left no art or artifacts that survive and are known only by the bits of tools and bone that have been found.

Home now to seven varieties of rattlesnakes and other

serious night crawlers. There is an almost perfect stillness over this now faintly starlit wasteland, and I think we all felt the aura of those ancient inhabitants of this very place upon us. – How different from us in their essence could they have been? Did they tell lies to each other and call them myth and/or belief? Did they use up today as if there were no tomorrows? — Succumb to a more or less constant death anxiety and remain at war with their own hearts? Or did they, in this vast open space, achieve a greater harmony with earth and sky, with their very soul breaths? — No answers in the great silence around us.

We fly back to New York just in time to catch the "Modernisms" exhibit of mid-twentieth century Turkish, Iranian and Indian art at NYU's Grey Gallery before it closes. Perhaps it was the memory of being in the Mojave at dusk, but the Indian artist Satish Gujral's "Christ in the Desert" immediately stops the visitor in his tracks. His Jesus, represented by a Cubist mask of a face, is asleep in what I take to be an oneiric version of the Judean wilderness. Violet shadows are thrown over the desert in such a way that they seem to emanate from the consciousness of this abstracted and supremely sad rendition of Christ. There are shadows that seem to pre-figure the cross and the image of a sliver of the actual cross to come.

Has he started his forty day fast?

Has he been tempted yet by that smooth talking Satan of the gospels of Matthew and Luke?

— There is only that disembodied mask to go on, with its thick unhappy parallel lines on both sides; its one oval eye faces us from the right and the merest asymmetrical suggestion of such an eye is on the left.

The mouth of the mask wears a deep frown, and we can only guess at the suffering that has gone into its creation. Perhaps its maker meant to convey a pain and bewilderment that can fairly make it seem as close to tears for us all.

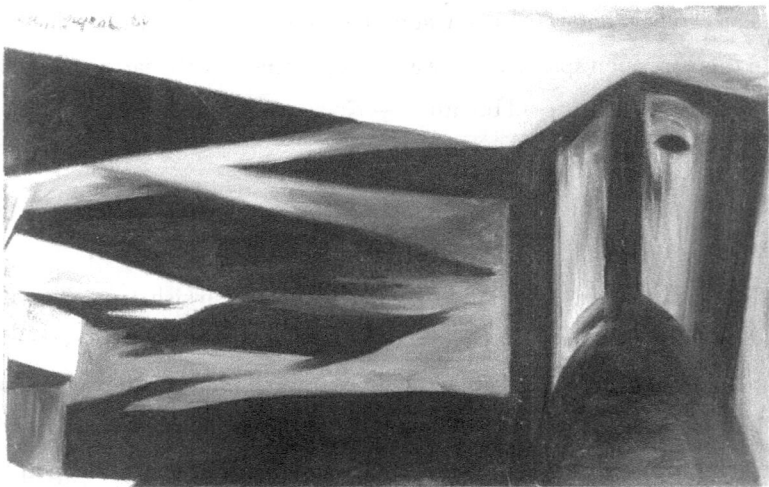

"The Self-Portrait, from Schiele to Beckmann" at the Neue Gallery (Featuring a Triptych by Felix Nussbaum)

I take the subway uptown on the Friday before the Memorial Day weekend to the plush converted townhouse digs of the Neue Gallery and commence drifting through Austrian/German variants on the ever-present Self.

Freakish/grotesque – artists' nightmares come to life in those
foreboding Teutonic cityscapes and private mirrors.

Myriad ways to present this haunted, contorted self of theirs
and ours:

Egon Schiele, the fluid, flitting early expressionist
extraordinary, voguing on the edge of the new century and oblivion.

Erech Heckel – *Portrait of a Man* (1919) – the epitome of
contemplative pain.

Herbert Bayer – Man as mannequin – art of *Humanly
Impossible* (1932).

Ernst Ludwig Kirchner – *Berlin Street Scene* (1913-14). The
algebra of need and everything that it is possible to buy and sell right
there before him. Is there a more perfect formula for catastrophe and
destruction?

Ludwig Meidner's *I and the City* (1913). "The world is out of
joint" (in his painting) the catalogist Rolf Johannsen notes. – Why, you
could make a case that the whole damn planet is exploding and his
psyche along with it.

Max Beckman's worldly alienation. – In that *Self-Portrait With
Horn* of 1938, grim and wary, his eyes seem to be straining futilely to see
their way around the corner and into the macabre future.

Haunted bastards, one and all. – And we are sure, in
retrospect, for the very best of reasons.

Felix Nussbaum's work takes us just far enough past 1940 that
we get close to the full measure of tragedy latent in the show as a
whole.

I wander over to the corner of the main exhibition room
where resides what is, in effect, if not conception, the triptych of his
end time.

1. *Self-Portrait in the Camp* (1940):

A ragged peakless cap, pronounced frown lines between his eyebrows. Grim, straight lips framed by his still young man's beard above his frayed shirt collar. – Not the shadow of an illusion left to call his own and the sky above dark with terrible intimations.

A man is shitting in a metal barrel behind him and a spectrally whitened inmate holding some sort of paper for his toilet is waiting his turn. – One of Primo Levy's Musselmen perhaps – that is, a person who has lost his will to live, in camp speak.

The painting is an extraordinary posting – bringing the past into the immediate future from an artist who was interned in Belgium when the Nazis invaded. Managing to escape, live with his wife and work for a short precious period of time, he rendered this unblinking picture of himself and the raw truth of the new Europe.

2. *Self-Portrait in a Shroud (Group Portrait)* (1942):

Three figures assembled behind him that seem fairly to represent aspects of the living Felix. Two of the three bear a close, if ghostly facial resemblance. They're both staring at their sallow fellow with his mouth agape, gripping a thick rope at its unraveling end. – A sort of shady brotherhood in group is how it appears.

The artist has a sprig of leaves between thumb and forefinger, which he holds with great delicacy while staring off to his right, quite ignoring us. The frown lines have appreciably deepened and his expression exquisitely mirrors the death anxiety inherent in his present moment and fatally truncated future.

3. *Self-Portrait with Jewish Identity Card* (1943):

Gallery goers drift over to the space where hangs the de

facto Nussbaum triptych. They whisper among themselves over the
Jew I.D. card. Hushed tones, always. – JUIF/JOOD. – Jew, you know,
they whisper. – A difficult subject, psychically and historically
touchy.

Big red letters: JUIF/JOOD. – "Sans" (patrie) written right
on the card by some miniscule bureaucrat. Sans – without. Yes, a
man without a country carrying a sealed fate. Staring out at us in
semi-profile, his yellow star above the right breast of his proper
overcoat.

Confined in a square, high-walled courtyard like a rat in a
trap. Take a good careful look is what the stare seems to be saying.

His whole family – mother, father, brother hunted down like
vermin and exterminated within a single year. He and his wife
disposed of at Auschwitz. – The wet dream of the new American
Nazis come true.

The furtive, cornered eye and its doomed shadows. –
Nothing for it. And excuse me, but what does Never Again fucking
mean, if it does not mean a call to arms here and now?

Rising above that courtyard in which he presents himself
and his I.D. is a tree with its branches sheared down to stumps. A few
boughs of white flowers show themselves next to that amputated
tree, along with a small patch of blue sky, posited in the catalog notes
as a sign of hope. But there's a cloud looming over that little patch of
light and the faint outline of black crows in flight over the menacing
expanse above him. Nothing about this painting leads me to believe
that the artist was kidding himself along even a tiny bit. – No, he's
cornered and gives himself to us as just that – a trapped specimen as
if under glass.

This is what it is to live and breathe with an invisible noose tightening around one's neck. – Yes, take a damn good look while you're at it. Much may depend upon it.

The saintly gaze of that figure in an invisible shroud displaced by the glittering eye that reflects the annihilating truth.

Behold this man, Nussbaum:

Black crows in flight;

Late twilight turns into

Deadbeat darkest night.

Painting After All

Gerhard Richter's *Painting After All*. – An exhibition at the
Met Breuer, March 4, 2020, and subsequently at the Metropolitan
Museum until January 18, 2021 – featuring *Birkenau*, abstractions
based on four photographs smuggled out of the Birkenau death camp
in 1944 [viewed online during the pandemic shelter-in-place at
metmuseum.org].

The accompanying text notes that in 2014 Richter revisited
sketches he had made of the photographs and painted them over "to
produce heavily disturbed, ruptured surfaces. This veiling holds in
tension the complex relationship of history and memory with the

forces of destruction and reconstruction, and with abstraction and representation." — In the world beyond museum speak, the viewer wonders if this has any currency whatsoever.

Painting After All –

Nobody has the right to proscribe, to affix judgment to true artistic expression; otherwise, it would be the death of art and that unfettered individual we call the artist. – A question as to what Richter brings forth in these abstractions, and, whatever it may be, mustn't we respect the desire not to merely create artifacts? — Those large-scale sketches of the Birkenau photos covered with paint and then literally squeegeed over so as to be something else again. – Abstract mirrors of the Unconscious made by an old man of great reputation with paint and time and perhaps, in his own mind, blood on his hands.

The Jew And The Abstract Truth:

The Jew himself as artifact / as obstacle to free breathing for the forward- looking post-war German. Can art exonerate, liberate the over-burdened creator's psyche? If such a way out isn't available to the layman, what is left to break those oppressive bonds but brazen denial, hatred, rationalization? — How much easier those haters and deniers must have it than their agonized countryman fiddling with the whole mess, painting things over one coat at a time.

Sonderkommandos – lit. "Operations" commandos. – Members of the Jew death squad (at Birkenau) who shepherded their brethren to the gas chambers, then shoveled their ashes and cleaned things up. Trading the lowest form of labor a Jew could perform for a bit more breath for themselves. Sonderkommando – a perfect Nazi euphemism. (See Victor Klemperer's <u>The Language of the Third</u>

Reich). – Jews acting in such a way with their tongue-in-cheek title. – The Nazis could point to them as one further proof of Jew degeneracy.

The four photos smuggled out of Birkenau that are the most explicit life and death proof of the existence of the gas chambers, taken by a death squad member at risk of instant execution or worse. The photos mounted along with Richter's Birkenau abstractions. "Retroactively [exposing] a thread of sorrow and guilt in the invariably subtle work of this German painter," according to the respected art critic Peter Schjeldahl.

Suppose we go whole hog and concede the Jew his unabashed humanity. What then? Why then there's a thorn in their side – we'll call it guilt – and what a drag, as we used to say, way back when. Guilty every time they take a good damn look – every time they allow themselves an unguarded thought.

What is an artist, a celebrated painter in his last innings to do? — What sort of heavily-layered smear can he conjure to obliterate the terrible unwritten laws of the soul?

> Layer it with coats of paint,
> many-colored.
> Leave it unrecognizable,
> somewhat beautiful.
> although maybe not so gorgeous
> as a clean slate.

Abstraction

of

what

exactly?

A blotting out of the four Birkenau photographs and their damning proof in favor of thickly-painted surfaces, polarities of thought and feeling...

Painting After All

Words not required – Not Birkenau – Not Jew – Not blood
— Not anything.
Absolutely entitled to paintings signifying nothing but themselves. –
A right to exist...

Once Richter uses *Birkenau* in his practice, certain questions
do arise...

The photos:

1) The march of naked stricken women to the gas chambers.
2) The shoveling of remains, ashes.
3) One squad member seems to walk a tightrope through a
   field of the dead while others engage in consultation.
4) Among the dead.

Should we allow for Richter's feelings being so overwhelmed that
these abstractions are his purest emotional response? Again, of
course, he is an artist free to express himself in whatever form he
wishes...

In Susan Tallman's "The Master of Unknowing" for the *New
York Review of Books'* May 14, 2020 issue, she quotes Richter as saying
that a good picture "takes away certainty because it deprives a thing
of its meaning and name. It shows us the thing in all the manifold
significance and infinite variety that precludes the emergence of any
single meaning and view." She adds that, "his work sets the will to
believe and the obligation to doubt in perfect oscillation."

The Jew as enigma to humankind – to the artist above all. –
Make him into a non-person, a cipher – a mystery not possible to
decode.

Cancel Him Out.

Tallman makes her liberal obsequies in regard to the
Sonderkommando photos: "Here meaning and name are
untouchable." — The name is intact – "Birkenau" – simple. The
essence of the meaning has indeed been touched and touched up
some more. Is no longer apparent to me. – A deliberate blur AFTER
ALL.

Of the Birkenau paintings she writes, "They are complex,
scarified" and also – here's the rub – "beautiful."

Before my very eyes on 9/11, nineteen years ago to the day
my pen is touching paper, the great orange fireball of the glittering
second tower against a perfect cobalt sky had a shocking aesthetic
death beauty. – A fact not decently to be dwelt upon.

Toward the conclusion of Tallman's essay: "The events of
1944 are beyond our reach. The subject of these paintings is not that
world, but our own – the place where we actively choose to know or
not know, see or not see..."

— The subject of these paintings is Richter's own
consciousness on which history has managed to insinuate a great
weight, despite his resistance of various sorts, early and in advanced
age. Here, in his after all, he paints what he can, given his belatedly-
announced subject and career-long obsession.

Does anyone really believe that this particular history is said
and done? — Violating as it does Wm. Faulkner's rubric that "The
past is never dead. It's not even past." Here, or in Germany, all you
need is the evidence of your senses.

Tallman's final take: "The story always changes with the
telling. Uncertainty is truth."

Did Richter wish for the Birkenau paintings to abet such

thinking as consonant with his artist convictions or his early belief
that he was guilt-free and that the burden of conscience his
generation labored under was mere posturing? — A deep
ambivalence, I think. – And a danger that in the process the truth can
magically disappear like so many Yiddish ghosts.

W.G. Sebald, an important German writer born in 1944,
explores the whole business of the war's aftermath and its
psychological consequences in his <u>On the Natural History of
Destruction.</u> An inquiry as to why an older generation of German
writers and artists "would not or could not describe the destruction of
German cities as millions experienced it." – Shame, guilt, the
humiliation of defeat occlude the view of the past. – Buried alive in
the deepest part of themselves. Can it be resurrected – brought into
clear focus? Or must some other sort of reality be superimposed?

Sebald offers his notes on the subject to "cast some light on
the way in which memory (individual, collective and cultural) deals
with experiences exceeding what is tolerable."

THE HORROR OF WAR

He relates a story he heard about a deranged woman fleeing
the bombing in Hamburg with a child's corpse in her suitcase.

Understandable, this evasion, memory erasure of these
terrors brought home. – Can a people accept the challenge to look
beyond their collective amnesia, dread, guilt? — To lift the veil a tiny
bit and then look fully with their eyes wide open?

In regard to his countryman, the pre-war novelist Alfred
Andersch, Sebald writes, "When a morally compromised author
claims the field of aesthetics as a value free area, it should make his
readers stop and think."

Aesthetics in "the after all" is the home base for the visual artist...still, it seems to me that the Jew never rises above the level of fossil in his concentration camp paintings. – No, I don't think Sebald, who was finely attuned to holocaust issues, would have been inclined to give Richter's *Birkenau* a pass.

In the foreword to the Destruction book, he puts it most precisely regarding his countrymen: "When we take a retrospective view, particularly of the years 1930 to 1950, we are always looking and looking away at the same time."

Benjamin H.D. Buchloh traces the obsessive thread of the artist's involvement with the Shoah in his essay "Documents of Culture, Documents of Barbarism, Richter's Birkenau Paintings" for the Metropolitan's catalog. – Six decades worth beginning in 1957 when, as a recent graduate of the Dresden Academy of Art, he made twelve anodyne drawings to illustrate an edition of The Diary of Anne Frank.

Grappling with "the question," according to Buchloh, "whether any artist, and more improbably any German painter, could possibly construct a credible mnemonic representation of the destruction of European Jews under the rule of German Nazi Fascism." — Mnemonic – an aid to memory – from the Greek for "mindful." And given all that, those European Jews of this Teutonic handwringing do not approach the Yiddish ghosts of I.B. Singer's Nobel acceptance speech – the descendants of poets and prophets who lovingly brought up their children and found "happiness where others [saw] nothing but misery and humiliation." — No, a mere trope, a creative conundrum in their rendering.

Der Hitler and a portrait of political prisoners being hung above a split image of movie starlets. – Richter painted them in 1963 after he had defected to the West and then destroyed both after his first group show in his new home.

In 1964-65 he did *Uncle Rudi* and *Aunt Marianne*, realistic portraits based on family photographs. – Uncle Rudi grinning in his Wehrmacht overcoat and cap before going off to be cannon fodder on the eastern front and Aunt Marianne, who had cradled him as a baby, then succumbed to schizophrenia and was starved to death under the Nazi fitness to live program. – A rubbing out of the weak, feeble minded, unproductive. – These works realistic and heartfelt. – The war come home in spades.

In the career-long Atlas that Richter maintained for conceptual sketches, he did several sheets of Euro pornography juxtaposed with concentration camp photos in 1967. – A puerile and obsessive exercise from a grown man. But all of a piece, evidently, with his stated obsession with these images from his student days.

Established as a leading artist in the reunited Germany, he was commissioned in 1997 to create towering panels for the entrance to the reconstructed Reichstag in Berlin. Richter fashioned one panel using rectangles of the German national colors and another of his by now ubiquitous concentration camp images. He finally rejected the latter concept (or gesture) and settled on six enameled glass panels in the colors of the flag.

It is stunning to me that he can't leave off the Jews. How, I ask myself, can he create that proper mnemonic that Buchloh believed he was striving to achieve with the voyeuristic exhibition of these starved and slaughtered victims stacked high? — How could it be that nowhere in his oeuvre do we find a single living Jew looking him and us in the eye? — That universal Jew who Joseph Goebbels claimed could be shamed just by detecting who and what he was? – When the artist can't literally or figuratively scrawl sorry over the

whole tragic mess? — That is, a sign of human contrition beyond
East Germany's state-sponsored self-righteous "memory culture" or
West Germany's open-handed reparations and conspicuous
memorials. – Something beyond mere fixation. Something nearer to
the artist and his art — in the vanguard of what is prototypically
thought of as human.

Obviously dissatisfied with what he had done up until that
time, Richter made large-scale sketches of the four photos smuggled
out of Birkenau in 2013. He then painted them over until they
evolved into those abstract paintings. Giving him his due, a wide
angle of the installation in Dresden shows the impressive breadth of
a world-class artist.

Buchloh very reasonably questions "whether and how
painterly abstraction could actually represent a fundamentally
unrepresentable historical subject." — And if "Art After All" is the
answer, we feel compelled to ask what is it an answer to?

Originally presented as simply *Four Abstract Paintings* at the
Dresden Albertinum in 2015, Buchloh writes that "only after a period
of additional reflection did the artist reluctantly decide to refer to
these works as the "Birkenau paintings." The four smuggled photos
were added to the exhibit, formally wedding them to the finished
paintings. – Whatever else there is to think, there was no letting go of
the subject for Richter.

These large-scale abstractions were created over a period of
three weeks in August 2014. Painting over the sketches of the
foundational photographs on the 2nd, 3rd, and 4th and again on the
13th and 14th, he appears to be striving for what he finally achieves on
the 25th with the last of the series. – A muted, complex blending of
colors that seems to mirror the emotional state of its creator. –

Provoking a reaction in the viewer in the way that living paintings do.

A beautiful picture if you choose to call it such. He did say he wished to make more than beautiful pictures. Could it be construed as a kind of against-the-grain interiority of atonement? — And was its purpose, whatever that purpose might have truly been, achieved? — A mystery, at least to me.

Atonement – originally to be at one with oneself, reconciled. And each soul lives and dies alone.

To Begin & End

Journal entry for 6/17/15:

     Yesterday, a few minutes after 7 p.m., a boy child was born into this world. – Son of my daughter and her husband. My Grandson.

     I commence reading <u>The Songs of Kabir</u> in the free-wheeling translation of Krishna Mehrotra. *

> "I beat on your door
> out of fear
> I wasn't yet born,
> I was in the womb
> when a great sadness
> came over me.
> It hasn't left me since
> it's with me now
> when I'm old and infirm
> and time shakes me by the hair.
>
> Time strikes the drum.
> I've nowhere to turn,
> Says Kabir. Let me in."

     Mehhrotra appends a note explaining this unspecified fear as the failure to find release from the cycle of birth and death. – In our terms, fear and sadness that there won't be a fix for the death anxiety that chokes off whatever life is naturally our own.

---

* <u>Songs of Kabir</u>, *New York Review of Books*, 2011

I think of my beloved grandson and the puzzle that we've all been given to solve, willy-nilly.

> "Listen, says Kabir.
> I have a prayer to make.
> I'm handcuffed to death.
> Throw me the key."

And

> "In the blink
> of an eye, says Kabir,
> the King will be separated from his Kingdom."

A further explication that the phrase "blink of an eye" goes back 3500 years to the <u>Rig Vida</u> and the <u>Ramayana</u>.

> The blink of an eye.
>
> The poor clueless time boy
>
> soldiers on.

> "In the end, says Kabir
> we're like a gambler
> who's lost his last penny.
> Standing at the edge of the road,
> He wrings his hands."

And

> "It's the same rope
> Ties us all,
> Though some appear bound
> Hand and foot
> And others free."

— How to explain this manifestly true statement?

All in the coils of mortality, alright, alright,

but a certain degree of difference in how we handle
this common fate.

First Rule:
    No self-congratulations in order.
    The same rope, the same fight for breath,
    the same old dust.

    The same confines (friendly and unfriendly)
And then, objectively what's left when we take it on down –
that is, Being pure and simple.

    This cellular knowledge of what is,
all that stands between us and rank metaphysical panic.

> "Listen [said] Kabir,
> I have a prayer to make.
> I'm handcuffed to death,
> Throw me the key."

Cuffed to death –
To the King's very own hardware. – Even Houdini, the great
magician and escape artist was ultimately baffled.

    He has a prayer to make, this mad bottom dwelling weaver,
son of a lowly weaver, who called himself the child of both Allah and
Ram. It's his overwhelming desire to unlock the most closely held
secret: forget those other chumps – this is he, this is me who follows
Rama.

> Free me up / turn me loose
> I'm beggin'.

(Kabir, whose body was fought over by Hindus and Muslims, both
wishing for the honor of conducting funerary rites for the great poet).

— The boy circumcised yesterday as black rain
clouds burst and lightning cracked in the best Cecil DeMille manner
over downtown Brooklyn.

Kabir, true aspirant to mystic union, juiced as he is in
Brahma and Rama, is also, as Evelyn Underhill points out in an
introduction to his work, always himself.

The subsumed individual consciousness
still breathes,
knows that it is knowing.

Even as he gives it up,
he asserts himself in words and music.

Kabir's Lord is King of the rhythm
of the heart.
In that rhythm of his, so frightening
to man on his bloody journey to no-self,
is the drumbeat of the renunciation of
the newly born, the newly dying.

And then there is the mystery of the essential shaping
utterance.
Kabir:
"From that word the world form has sprung,

that word reveals all.

But who knows whence the word cometh?"

He bums around in the back alleys of mere knowledge,
aches in his emptiness for a map of the way home.

At the end, Kabir says

"My heart is dying, though it lives."

— Why does Mr. K. sing and jabber so?

Perhaps because the true poet, our special envoy, is even
more terrified than the rest of us ordinary Joes.

The King of Terrors

pursues him into every corner,

won't let him off his flaming hook.

Kabir approaches his Lord as a bride in many of his poems.
– as a lovelorn bride.

Advice to the lovelorn desperately seeking...

No sense in false blustery Trumpian

pride – damn, we're down to just beggin'.

Man to Man:
the Enigma of Vaslav Nijinsky —
Part One

<u>With Robert Wilson On the Train To Yonkers –</u>

Eighteen months in 1969-70 as the extremely unlikely director of the Messiah Baptist Church Head Start program at 76 Warburton Ave., Yonkers, NY. Just back from teaching Principles of Education at Maru Teachers College, way up north in Nigeria, where the dry savannah begins turning into the Sahara Desert.

Fresh I was, pretty much — the small black church is riven over whether to continue its pre-school and social work program. – Class differences, friction on the church board, egoistic politics. I'm somehow settled upon. Federal dollars allow for a per diem educational consultant. A friend of a friend recommends Robert Wilson. He has a background in special education back in Texas, is just getting started with his career in NY and can use the dough. We take the train up to Yonkers maybe a half dozen to a dozen times. He does marvelous creative things with our three and four-year-olds. I sometimes wonder if any of those pre-schoolers or their parents know that a world class genius of theater and dance was working with them back then. Someone with the ability to turn the stage into a magical box and come close to suspending time in space.

On the nearly hour-long rides out of Grand Central he talked rather compulsively, as I recall, about Nijinsky's last dance – that dance of life that was pregnant silence and that dance of death that was the violence that he did to himself until he was brought to a halt. In Wilson's telling, Nijinsky threw himself about the stage and beat himself to a bloody pulp until he was taken away to an asylum. Maybe I have the details wrong, or maybe he did, but that was the poetic essence of what he said and a fair approximation of what actually happened.

There is an announcement of his coming production of "Letter to a Man" in October 2016 at BAM where we saw that brave, lonely production of "Einstein On The Beach" while he was still working with us in Yonkers. Something I feel I should really catch – like the end of an interrupted monologue from another lifetime. Prepare by reading Nijinsky's <u>Diary Of Life And Death</u> which commences just after the terrifying performance outside St. Moritz on Jan.19,1919. There is also that "Letter To Man" addressed to his nemesis, the impresario Sergei Diaghilev, appended to the unexpurgated edition of the diary published in English in 1999. The Diary famous as the living record of a great artist's desperate struggle to hold on to his disintegrating consciousness since its original publication in 1934.

<u>Dance Of Life And Death</u>

Nijinsky writes "I am afraid of death and therefore do not want it." [*]

and

"I love everyone, but I am not loved."

and

"My movements are simple."

---

[*] All Nijinsky quotations from <u>The Diary of Vasllav Nijinsky</u>, Unexpurgated Edition, translated from the Russian by Kyril Fitzlyon. Ed. Joan Acocella. NY: Farrar, Straus & Giroux, 1999.

Forty odd years before privileged to watch R. Wilson in studio with acolytes. – His movements were also simple and direct.

Simple movements the foundation of both men's art. With Nijinsky we can see in the miniscule amount of film that has been preserved that they arise purely and deeply from his heart and soul, so that the world was brought to breathless awe and amazement.

He tells us that he chased after "tarts" before and during marriage while maintaining a close, if shifting, relationship with God who has increasingly mixed messages for him. The distinction that he makes most clearly is between artists and non-artists, rich or poor.

"I want to write this book because I want to explain what feeling is." – Surrounded by persons in his household including his precious wife, who seems to him to be without that quality he knows to be true feeling.

"I am a man like Christ who fulfills God's commands." – The fine psychic line between being "like Christ" and believing himself to be Christ will dangerously blur and disintegrate in the six weeks of the Diary's composition. And the question does arise that if Jesus had not been terminated for his indiscretions, might he too have possibly self-destructed as did Nijinsky in his relative purity and innocence.

In writing about charitable institutions, his hot and tempting sister-in-law Tessa, the poor, the aftermath of the war, the environment of the planet, Nijinsky displays great insight as well as overwhelming naiveté and that growing derangement.

Thinking back over the years, with the Diary in front of me, and somewhat, although not a great deal less ignorant than when we took those train rides up to Yonkers, it seems to me that Robert

Wilson in his belief and absorption in his talent, shrewdness and
innocence, bore a certain resemblance to Nijinsky and knew it —
even a faint facial likeness.

"Words are not speech. I understand speech in all
languages." – But communication with psychiatrists and caregivers in
languages other than Russian will prove close to the core of his
coming difficulties. Claims to understand the Hungarian spoken by
his wife and Tessa. – Speech – sound – he understands/intuits the
souls of people, he believes.

"I like dirty Jews who have lice on their bodies. I know that
if they listen to me, they will agree that I am right. They will obey
and understand me... I am a Jew by origin, for I am Christ. A Jew is
not Christ, for he is a Jew." — Ah well, no more two-headed than the
rest of the western world.

Dirty Jew.

I was one once. Humiliated, neglectful of my person and
neglected.

Not Christ-like, because we imagine Jesus as virtuously
clean about his person.

Imagine him spiritually focused and not diffuse. – But it
takes more than just suffering to be Christ-like, and we know him to
be the subject of all sorts of failed aspirations and identifications.

"I am god and man. I am what Christ felt. I am Buddha and
every kind of God."

He feels. The world does not feel. – A dangerous path
has opened up.

"My madness is love for people." — Doesn't mention that
he parades the town with a huge gold cross around his neck,
exhorting the residents of St. Moritz to go to church. Doesn't

mention the incident when he drives a sleigh dangerously into traffic or the pushing of his wife down a staircase with his truly beloved daughter Kyra in her arms.

"I want to be called God and not Nijinsky..."

"I am hunger. I am the man who does not die of hunger..."

A myriad of crayon drawings done during the composition of the Diary. Striking angry circular eyes all over the place. He tells his wife Romola that they are a soldier's face and the drawings are for the war, but we can see that the drawings were an immensity beyond that. Romola later wrote that they made her shudder. And she has her reasons. Right after that final public performance of Jan. 1919, a young doctor is brought in from one of the fancy resorts in town for consultation in Nijinsky's case and quickly becomes her lover. How much her husband knew and how much he intuited is a critical question, but those bug-eyed drawings must have seemed to follow her everywhere.

That legendary final performance before around two hundred invited guests and whoever else could jam into the ballroom of Suvretta House, a hotel in a pine woods outside town.

We have a description of sorts by Romola, never a fully reliable witness, and some remarks by the great dancer as well. Romola:

"Nijinsky began by taking a chair, sitting down in front of the audience, and staring at them for what seemed like half an hour. Eventually he unrolled two lengths of velvet, one white, one black, to form a cross on the floor. Standing at the head of the cross, he addressed the audience: 'Now I will dance you the war.... the war which you did not prevent.' He then launched into a violent solo, presumably improvised, and at some point stopped." Nijinsky wrote that he wanted to dance more, but God said to him "Enough."

After the performance, Romola commented that she never felt the same again (about their relationship we can assume). Clearly the waters had gotten too deep. – What had she gotten herself into? An intimation that her husband and his art were way beyond her control or understanding.

In the diary Nijinsky writes, "The audience came to be amused. They thought I was dancing to amuse them. I danced frightening things. They were frightened of me and therefore thought I wanted to kill them." The audience gets restless and he began to "play" cheerful things and the audience laughed. Then he "danced badly because I kept falling on the floor" when he didn't have to.

He mingles with the guests afterwards and has what must have been a disastrous conversation with an aristocratic lady about prostitution. Shows her lascivious movements and his bloodied foot. Later, on their way home in their carriage he tells his wife:

"Today was the day of my marriage to God." — The event that Robert Wilson talked about. His bloody, beaten feet – the bloody instruments of his spontaneous, unmediated art. Only the audible voice of God seems to have kept him from beating himself to death before his well-heeled, cold-hearted audience.

> The besieged, frightened, martyred
>   self
> Suffering Jesus and omniscient God Almighty all in one,
>   but not without a few wretched doubts.
> The voices heard in the corner of the eyes,
>   the eyes resembling female genitalia.

<u>What's a man to do?</u>
— Ashamed most of all that he lives and breathes –
        The cracked heart and mind of the cuckold
        of all time.

A hardly disguised lust for sister-in-law Tessa.
Romola wrote how her husband, taught Tessa how to walk. Knew precisely, as they all did, just what it was he wished to teach Tessa.

      Dr. Curt Frenkel and Romola – Nijinsky notes that they speak some secret language – here he seems to know everything and yet hides it from himself. – Cannot say to himself what it is that he knows while writing the diary. – A split.

      For this poor fellow, used, dominated, passed around among older, monied Russian aristocrats as a youth, wished most fervently to be a man against all odds. Married the young Hungarian woman, Romola de Pulszky in Buenos Aires in September 1913 after she pursued him aboard a ship bound for his performances in South America. Married the smitten woman impulsively after barely exchanging a few words with her. Diaghilev, the imperious master of the Ballets Russes, was said to have fainted dead away when he heard of this betrayal by his protégé and erstwhile lover. He proceeded to drop him from the company and effectively leave him and his family, which would come to include a young daughter, without either financial or artistic resources.

      Now, isolated in a chalet on a hill in St. Moritz, taking his meals in his room while Romola dallies with Dr. Frenkel, he is still manly in his attentions to his young sister-in-law.

      "Tessa feels me because I give her a lot of presents. Besides this, Tessa feels music and dancing and understands everything I do.... I know her habits. She likes men. She gets drunk with them. She is a bad woman because she has many habits. I am a bad man because I do things together with other people. God wanted me to understand Tessa."

The ideation is veiled, breaks up, wanders, but his desire for Tessa, her leading him on and his peculiar inhibitions self-evident and ultimately self-destructive.

———————

"Lloyd George [British Prime Minister and chief negotiator for his country at the Paris talks that led to the signing of the Treaty of Versailles in June 1919] is a terrible man. I do not like terrible men. I will not harm them. I do not want them to be killed. They are eagles. They prevent small birds from living, and therefore one must guard against them." — A tangle of contradictory thoughts follow. – A cocktail of fear, guilt, shame that leads to the obliteration of the coherent self and its diffusion on the printed page. Of course, his insights into the catastrophe of the treaty would prove correct, but it is the mystery of those tragic elements in Nijinsky, that shattering loss of control, his impotence on the cusp of his terrible fate that grips us in the reading of the Diary.

The eminent doctors who would make learned pronouncements, their chicken shit menu of categories, prognoses, judgments. The system rigged, the deck stacked, the fix in.

Poor Nijinsky!

Dostoyevsky's The Idiot and his innocent Prince Myshkin.

Nijinsky has read this tale, relates to both the author and his martyred prince.

Nijinsky in regard to Lloyd George and Diaghilev:

"It is not for me to be their judge, but for God. I am God

and I will tell them the truth." – A prototypical thought movement in the Diary.

"My wife does not love me or the work. I understand my wife. I know her habits. She likes being polite." – A devastating, laconic take on his old lady who he has pinned, despite other professions of love for her.

References to Dostoyevsky's <u>The Idiot</u> run through the Diary: Prince Myshkin is surrounded by complex intrigues way beyond the parameters of his innocent understanding. – Sexual and financial intrigue/class and political intrigue. Quite a bit going on in the Nijinsky household as well.

Dr. Frenkel, his new great friend, shows Nijinsky erotic Japanese "pillow books" to discover his sexual fantasies during what amounted to an amateur psychoanalysis. – Banging Romola at the same time. Seems to have found himself in love with her. According to the story that was passed down in his family and told to Joan Acocella in the 1990's, he attempted suicide by drug overdose in 1920 when she wouldn't divorce Nijinsky and marry him and was rescued by his wife. He remained a morphine addict until his death from pneumonia at the age of 51 in 1938. Although the time sequence is somewhat unclear, he continued to play a crucial role in the martyring of the great artist during the following years of his forced confinement.

Meanwhile, in those last weeks before Nijinsky is locked away, he lavishes gifts on Tessa as she attempts to seduce him. Graphic in the Diary:

"She loves a prick. She needs a prick. I know pricks who do not love her."

Deep in his increasingly disordered mind, he doesn't seem

ready to admit to himself, or at least commit to the written page, his
deep attraction to this "polluted" Tessa of his. A most confused
muddle, as is his general bisexual ambivalence. Part of the great
ongoing drama that played itself out in St. Moritz and led to the
ultimate destruction of the God of the Dance.

He is really wise to Dr. Frenkel and Romola and their plans
to institutionalize him: "I feel in advance what will happen to me if
God abandons me. I know that if God abandons me, I will die." —
And, of course, he was eventually abandoned by, or abandoned
himself, or simply lost to God. – Take your pick.

"I do not want to go mad and therefore will do everything for
the sake of their (Frenkel and Romola's) health.

"Then that saddest bravado:

"I'm not Nijinsky, as they all think. I am God in man."

And with great, if temporary clarity, writing of himself in the
second person: "If people want to judge you, you will say that
everything you say is said by God. Then you will be sent to a lunatic
asylum."

He believes the voice of God speaks the simple truth to him:

"God is beauty with feeling."

In the dance he passes this particular test of divinity with
ease.

――――――――

A base reality seeps into his consciousness and his writing: "I
can no longer trust my wife, for I have felt that she wants to give these
notebooks to Dr. Frenkel to examine." And with the threadbare
dignity he tries to maintain here, and in his coming letter to
Diaghilev: "I love my wife. She loves me, but she thinks Dr. Frenkel
is God. Dr. Frenkel is not God. I am."

The Diary has a precious, even sacred value to him:

>"I cannot weep, for fear that my tears will fall on
my notebooks."

Letter (within the text of the Diary) to Frenkel: "I know that I will be
forced to go away. I know that my luggage is already packed." — He
is, finally, powerless against the forces arrayed against him. There is
no one near who is for him, and he cannot muster the strength or
focus to be for himself.

>"I almost wept when he [Dr. Frenkel] told me he was my
friend." Nijinsky will emphatically change his mind on this subject,
but long after what may be considered the lowest sort of betrayal,
and after the damage is irreparable.

>He is taking his meals in his room when Tessa leaves for her
home in Vienna and he does weep. An isolated invalid in the
mountain of Switzerland is what he has become. A sense of
impending crucifixion – the aspiration and identification with Jesus
— the sense that martyrdom was at least partially wished for. – And
the other players, wife, Frenkel, summoned from Vienna mother-in-
law, father-in-law, all ready to accommodate him.

>A ritual series of movements toward Zurich
and the grisly revelation of his fate.

>Why, we could set it to music
and make an even greater bloody dance.

>A dance to recapitulate the deadly truth he had revealed to
the swells that Sunday afternoon at Survetta House, only longer,
slower, leaning toward the infinitely, inevitably malign.

>"I am a lunatic with a mind, and therefore my nerves are
trained. I am nervous when I want to be nervous. I am not nervous

when I must convince people I am not nervous."

The self-professed lunatic tells himself that he controls his
own fate. – It is all in a moment – a puff of psychic smoke.
"God is fire in the head. I am alive as long as I have a fire in
my head."

              The ragged burning fire
              In the head of Vaslav Nijinsky.

              So scary and repellant to the world
                around him. Scary and at times repellant
                  to him too, we can be quite sure.
"I read <u>The Idiot</u> when I was eighteen and understood its meaning."

(The innocent, Prince Myshkin, destroyed by the perversity,
evil cynicism around him.)

"When I read <u>The Idiot</u>, I felt that the Idiot was not an idiot
but a good man. I could not understand <u>The Idiot</u> because I was still
too young. I now understand Dostoyevsky's Idiot because people
take me for an idiot."

The good/saintly man, Prince Myshkin, was vulnerable in
ways that Nijinsky clearly understood and took as his own.
Although he is struggling mightily to keep a tenuous grip on reality
in this latter portion of the Diary, there are moments of great
penetration. References to his struggling youth with his mother
when the family lacked for bread and his early encounters with
Diaghilev driven by necessity. Then incisively: "I know that nervous
people are subject to madness and therefore I was afraid of madness.
I am not mad, and Dostoyevsky's Idiot is not an idiot." — But Prince
Myshkin is finally and permanently incapacitated by the homicidal

predilections of the world.

It is Nijinsky's ambition to go to Paris (where peace talks among the great powers are taking place over the terms and conditions of the end of the great war) and help President Wilson and "Wilsonism" overcome the global madness.

Largely self-taught, Nijinsky commented on the folly of harsh peace terms with Germany and correctly predicted a recurring catastrophe. He believed in Wilson and aspired to aid the American president in negotiating a just peace.

<u>Letter to a Man</u> –

It was at this point, according to Acocella, the editor of the unexpurgated edition of the Diary, that Nijinsky broke off his narrative and began a series of letters to friends, to the President of the Council of Allied Forces, finally in letters fifteen and sixteen to Mankind and Jesus. The Wilson/Baryshnikov piece Letter to a Man is concerned with the crucial ninth letter to his former lover, the impresario of the ground-breaking Ballets Russes, Sergei Diaghilev. It has the salutation "To Man" and then "I cannot call you by name because you cannot be called by your name. I am not writing to you quickly because I am not a nervous man." — (A sort of clearing of the throat in addressing the awesome personage who shaped his life and career and whom he has clearly not yet fully escaped.)

Certain compare and contrasts he makes between himself and the man whose protégé and lover he was for five years before his marriage in 1913:

"You are a man with intelligence and without feeling.... You want to destroy me. I want to save you." He alludes to the nature of their past psycho-sexual relationship that began when he was

eighteen and Diaghilev was seventeen years his senior. A past that
for Nijinsky seems always to be in the present tense, "I know your
tricks. I pretended to be stupid. I was not a kid. I was God. I am God
within yourself. You are a beast, but I am love."

An avatar he insists, even during his humiliated, sexually
exploited youth with Diaghilev and other wealthy Russian
aristocrats. Then a series of variations on

"You are mine/I am yours"

and a repetition of the basic accusation along with an odd declaration
of fidelity:

"You are the one who calls for death

I am yours, but you are not mine."

There follows a lengthy defense of his manhood that seems to stand
against all that came before:

"I am a prick, but not yours –

....

I am the prick, I am the Prick

I am God in my prick

....

You are a prick, but not the Prick

I can prick, prick

You cannot prick a prick (and we take this as heartfelt)

I am a prick in His Prick."

(A godly prick as it were).

A last paragraph to Diaghilev in prose with a nursery rhyme-
like "Sleep in peace, rockabye, bye. Bye. Bye. Bye."
And the meant-to-be straight from the shoulder closing —

                              Man to Man
                              Vasla v Nijinsky

This all from a ghost letter that was never mailed, perfectly mirrors his spirit of futile defiance. – Although I may have been used as a woman and now find myself in terrible straits, I am a man, you see.

In the theatrical reading of the letter, Wilson/Baryshnikov crucially omit that "Man to Man sign off, for whatever reason. A letter to himself really, buried in the fourth notebook. Noble as well as damaged – from the dust of his degraded, poverty-stained, personal history."

Later, in the Diary: "I noticed my mistake, as I wrote the name of god and of Diaghilev with a capital letter. I will spell god with a small letter because I want to make a distinction."

Wrenching himself back from the terribly mistaken apprehension that Diaghilev was godlike. A separation between that man and a god or God that he must make clear to himself. – Still so painful that at a certain point in time in their relationship, it was not at all certain that the powerful impresario was not godlike. – A distinction he must absolutely make now for the sake of his fragile sense of who and what he has become.

Writing of an incident some years previously when he contracted typhoid fever and was helpless, he describes the process whereby he is persuaded that he must live with Diaghilev and be taken care of at the negotiated price of his body and soul.

"I was afraid of Diaghilev and not of death."

Diaghilev took control of his life and would keep a tight hold until his precipitous marriage to Romola Pulszky in 1913 and the break. Of course, no need for the letter "To Man" or for the commentary if he were still not in his grip one way or another.

He has a falling out with Romola and uses the Diary to air

the essence of his grievance with her:

"You have called Dr. Frenkel. You have trusted a stranger and not me.... He is afraid of showing his wife that he is nothing. Nothing, because everything that he has learned by studying is nothing.... I do not want to dance the way I used to, because all those dances are death. Death is not only when the body dies. The body dies, but the spirit lives. The spirit is a dove, but in God. I am God, and I am in God.... You do not want to go on walks with me. You think I am ill. You think that because Dr. Frenkel told you I was ill."

He ends this letter in a devotional poetic form that devolves into a mystifying doggerel that must have frightened Romola even more. He leaves the house and heads for town, lightly dressed for the winter chill and with just a little money in his pocket. He sees Dr. Frenkel heading toward their house and realizes that Romola has called for him because his behavior has again alarmed her.

"I went on with a bowed head as if guilty of something." — Guilty of being fully alive – of knowing too much and too little.

He looks unsuccessfully for some sort of shelter or lodging, goes higher and higher in the mountains, is near to freezing to death. He sees a horse being made to run uphill:

"I realized that people urged horses and men on until they stopped and fell like stones. The horse and I decided they could whip us as much as they wanted, but we would still do what we liked, because we wanted to live. The horse walked and so did I."

He descends to the village of St. Moritz where Frenkel catches up with him and escorts him home.

He again writes to his wife:

> "I want to tell you that you are death
> and I am life

....

You do not love me you

I love I love you"

He has behaved toward her and perhaps others in the household in such a way as to make them think he is mentally ill. Perhaps a little rougher with the maid when he came in out of the cold than he lets on. His wife is weeping upstairs with Frenkel attentively at her side.

Crucially, he writes "My soul is sick. My sickness is of the soul and not the mind."

In the whole sordid medical/psychiatric record that would be compiled over the next thirty years, and which is carefully examined in the psychiatrist Peter Ostwald's <u>A Leap Into Madness</u>, there does not appear to have been anyone ready and able to engage with his soul, empathize with its loss of bearings – even speak to him in his own Russian language.

"My sickness is too great for me to be cured of it too soon. I am incurable.... I am a man and not God .... I am God. I am a man. I am a man and not a beast."

Ends Book I "The Book of Life" on Feb. 27, 1919 with the thought that he is seeking God and God is seeking him. On the same day he begins Book II "On Death." It will end on Mar. 4, about a week later, with his being taken to Zurich for psychiatric treatment and confinement that will last for most of the rest of his enigmatic and tragic life. Opening of the Death Book simple and terrible:

"Death came unexpectedly, for I wanted it.... I have been told that I am mad. I thought that I was alive. They would not let me alone."

and

"I am the God who dies when he is not loved."

and

"People who have lost their reason are called extinguished." — A crisis of will and belief.

He calls himself a beast and a predator and wants to make love to prostitutes and live like an unnecessary man. – the sexual guilt comes from a mysterious place, the pressing against the boundaries of that guilt only natural. The desire to sink into the superfluous as in the underground of desperate characters in Dostoyevsky, Turgenev and Gorky we'll take to be intrinsic to his cultural patrimony.

There are guilty admissions of lusts for animals, his daughter, his famous actress of a mother-in-law. The wish to be committed to an asylum.

When his wife moved out of the bedroom they shared: "I am sorry for myself and for her. I am weeping. I am cold. I do not feel. I am dying. I am not a God. I am a beast." —This is awful. – It is as if he is in the coils of those terrible twin serpents that strangled Laocoön and his children before the gates of
Troy.

I am God/I am not God

(the lunatic conundrum)

and the compelling question:

Who and what am I really?

Finally,

What is a man?

The question reverberates from that heartfelt bedrock letter to Diaghilev. –That terrible, frightening and unanswerable question that haunted Prince Myshkin as well.

"I am a beast....I have sharp claws." He will tarry at home, drink alcohol and eat meat contrary to his instincts and Tolstoyan principles, this man/beast.

Isolated in his room upstairs, he hears the conspiratorial murmur of his wife and newly summoned-in-a-crisis in-laws below.

"I want to laugh, because I felt laughter, but I understood death and stopped."

That feeling from the deep well of the psyche that if laughter begins, it will not end – that consciousness will disintegrate, that the very self will dissolve until there is just that cosmic laughter in the void. – Rather like that night at Hong Fat's Restaurant on Mott St. long ago when I scooped noodles from my empty bowl into a girl named Sally's empty bowl. – A real endless howler if I let it become one, until I slowly chewed it on down to the acid truth and survived the rest of that infinitely slippery night.

"I know what life is. I know what death is. The sun is reason. The intellect is an extinguished sun that is decomposing."

and presciently,

"The earth is suffocating. There is not enough air for it."

————————————

"I know that many people will say that Nijinsky is a crybaby. I am not a dying man. I am alive and therefore I suffer."

> A tortured, persecuted cuckold,
> An artist whose downfall
>   Is being plotted as he lives and breathes.
> Master of the truth of the dance,
>   he is not a crybaby, although one
>   must be made of stone not to weep
>   at what is to become of him.

"I am afraid of intelligent people. They smell of cold. I freeze when I have a man with a brain next to me. I am afraid of intelligent people because they smell of death." — Intellectuals divorced from their bodies and souls. Stilted, at least once removed from life as opposed to free creative individuals.

"God is not in icons. God is in the soul of man. I am God. I am the spirit."

And, of course, the Diary endures because it is, despite its anomalies, a strikingly real spiritual document.

"People can kill me, but I will still live because I am everything. I want eternal life. I do not want death."

In summation:

"I am the spirit in every man.

I am Nijinsky."

Baryshnikov gives tremendous Russian linguistic emphasis to these words in the play – as if the man Nijinsky were staggering under the monumental weight of his vey name. – As if he were trying to create a whole being out of his fragmented psyche by the talismanic invocation of it. And this leads to another possible articulation of the "Nijinsky" of the Diary – soft, hopeful, fearfully, tentatively insistent in its iteration.

He gets a fix on his physician/rival. Meat-eating, chain-smoking Curt Frenkel, a fresh knight in the great establishment citadel of sanity. Nijinsky writes that he hid his diaries in the piano "because I was sure that Dr. Frenkel would not understand them and take me for a madman." Frenkel had taken courses in medical school with Dr. Ernest Bleuler who had originally coined the term "schizophrenia" for a variety of associated mental illnesses and the term "schizophrenic" would cling to Nijinsky over the years with much greater tenacity than precision. Frenkel would direct Nijinsky to Bleuler in Zurich and was, in fact, central to the drama being played out, but in the two books that would be published under Romola Nijinsky's name about her husband and his history and condition, he is never mentioned once. There is a picture of him at forty in the Acocella edition of the Diary. Rather dapper in suit and bowtie, with his eyes downcast and his manicured hand to his mouth. Conventionally handsome. Not capable of comprehending, it seems to me, who and what he contributed to destroying.

Of his in-laws, the other players in the crisis enveloping the Nijinsky household, he writes, "I am afraid of Oscar and Emma. They are both dead." Emilia Markus and her second husband Oscar Pardany already have a complicated history with their son-in-law in Budapest, when he was confined as an enemy alien in their home for eighteen months during what we now call World War I. No thanks for what passed for hospitality when he, Romola and their daughter Kyra are sprung on a special visa to the then neutral United States for a tour with Diaghilev's Ballets Russes in 1916. Very little goodwill toward their troublesome son-in-law and Nijinsky certainly felt and returned the chill.

Frenkel's loyalties compromised as he administers tranquilizers and prepares his patient for transport to Dr. Bleuler. Romola, semi-hysterical, servants openly weeping as they go to and fro. The stage is set.

The Night Before Zurich –

A comment that Nijinsky made in his "Letter To Man": "I

like people. Dostoyevsky liked people. I am not an idiot. I am a
human being."

In <u>The Idiot</u>, the argumentative character, Ippolit, finds no
contradiction between Prince Myshkin being extremely intelligent
and "an idiot – without doubt – after all is said and done." And that is
the thing about idiots and holy men. – Men who cannot help being
who they are. – As opposed to ordinary men who mold themselves to
circumstances.

Nijinsky (nearing the end of his diary): "I want to describe
my life as an artist." He proceeds to discuss his masturbatory habits
from age nineteen, Paris "tarts" and "Jeux", his early ballet involving
the flirtatious play of two young women and a man. He states that
the ballet was based on Diaghilev's repeated fantasy of making love
to two boys at the same time, which he found repellent. He details
his interactions the day before with his mother-in-law. Finds her
very clever, although he clearly loathes and fears her. Says she
reminds him of Diaghilev. A wicked woman he wishes removed
from the face of the earth. But for all the loathing, we wonder if he
considered for a moment the deep concealed truth that she and her
husband Oscar were there to do Romola's bidding. – To help in the
work of his removal at her request.

Then, in a note of terrible resignation: "I know that I must go
to Zurich tomorrow and will therefore go to bed now." At this point,
we feel at both a visceral and rational level, he knows that he is going
to his doom. – Somehow powerless to prevent it. As if his will is
paralyzed, and he is to be a spectator at his own crucifixion.

A fatal entanglement with Romola that would turn into a
mad indifference and rage over the years of his coming confinement.
How could he have been so helpless in dealing with the stilted,

materialistic woman that she reveals herself to be in the biographies that she would subsequently publish about her husband? His dreadful entanglements with God and his old lady, his stumbling block of a self.

Then the awful pre-arranged moment:

"My wife came to me," he writes "and told me that I should tell Kyra I would not be coming back.... I said if she was not afraid of me I would not remain in Zurich, but that if she was afraid of me I would prefer to be in a lunatic asylum because I am not afraid of anything." — And we know that he wholly loved and doted on daughter Kyra and that Romola was a cold-hearted and indifferent mother on her best days. We have her own words for this as well as Kyra's testimony. – Yes, innocent he was and self-sacrificing to the point of martyrdom, this transcendent artist of whom the critic and eye witness, Cyril Beaumont, wrote, "Always he appeared to be part of a race apart, of another essence than ourselves ..."

As the Diary closes, he again drifts into his political obsessions, his feeling that Britain's Lloyd George is the villain of the negotiations in Paris and that Woodrow Wilson represented man's better instincts. For some reason believes that France's Clemenceau, the most implacable advocate for punitive peace terms with Germany, will translate his written pacifist sentiments into French when he sees them.

"I will show Lloyd George that I am man-God. Come on out. Come on out and fight with me. I will defeat everyone. I am not afraid of bullets and prison. I am afraid of spiritual death. I will not go insane, but I will weep and weep. I am a man. I am God."

That on-going debate with himself whether God/god is upper or lower case.

Man/God   God/god

Nearing the end of the Book of Death with Zurich looming over him and he raises the stakes: "I feel the Earth is suffocating, and therefore I ask everyone to abandon factories and obey me. I know what is needed for the salvation of the earth."

and

I am the Divine Savior. I am Nijinsky and not Christ. I love Christ because he was like me."

Is there a formula here? Every humiliation, threat to his manhood, danger of obliteration leads to more grandiose claims of divinity, prophetic vision. – And, of course, humanly, in the midst of a drowning confusion, he saw and intuited a great deal. – The callous slaughter of mankind and the indifference of the idle rich, the desecration of the living planet. There is also a question as to how he experienced his own on-rushing disintegration and the betrayal that went along with it.

The end of the Notebook On Death:

I will go now ....

I am waiting ....

I do not want ....

"I will go to my wife's mother and talk [is he actually looking for mercy from her and her crew?] – because I do not want her to think that I like Oscar more than her. I am checking her feelings. She is not dead yet because she is envious."

....

Oh, how wistful and lost he is in what is called a state of madness. – Cold blood and stone and barely a human twitch around him. — A man who could see, feel, create from the deepest part of himself.

The Idiot

Prince Myshkin on the moments before his epilepsy seized him:

"Thinking of that moment later, when he was alright again, he often said to himself that all of these gleams and flashes of the highest sensation of life and self-consciousness, and therefore also of the highest form of existence, were nothing but disease, the interruption of the normal condition: and if so, it was not at all the highest form of being, but on the contrary must be reckoned the lowest."

Nijinsky's mental illness, certain far-seeing aspects of it, pose a similar paradox –

The epileptic "idiot" / the lunatic seer who identified closely with his fictional counterpart.

Studies in aspects of the nature of innocence.

———————————

He will go now – the next morning, Nijinsky and Romola, his son-in-laws and Dr. Frenkel are off to Zurich and the fated meeting with the pioneering Dr. Bleuler. As he is trundled into a railroad car for the four-hour ride and as the wheels clack on the railroad bed, does he remember his summary lines written to his friend, the Uruguayan diplomat and writer Andre de Badet:

"I am a man for God. I am a man for him. I love Him very much. I am a man. I am a man."

Like a rebellious and insistent Delta blues singer
in an abyss of oppression and humiliation: I'm a man.
Whatever else they try to make of me,
I'm a man!

———————————

Flight – Ancillary

"Nijinsky had always been famous for his jump. As witnesses describe it, he would rise and then pause in the air before coming down. Now, it seemed, he had declined to come down."

— J. Acocella

(A professional intellectual 's lame-ass aperçu.)

The great athletic leapers – Michael Jordan and those who came before and after him – all created at least the visual effect of a pause at the top of their jumps. Nijinsky also seems to have believed that he took a brief rest at his apex before returning to the ground.

My own dreams of levitation:

1) I would rise and incredibly, by a terrible act of will, stay two feet or so off the ground until I felt my head and heart would burst, then would wake up before sure death.

2) A basketball in my hands, I would rise and pump and double and triple and quadruple pump, ready to shoot my jump shot – just treading air and for some unfathomable reason unable to get the shot off.

There could have been holy dreams of levitation on Nijinsky's part, but I do not believe that he deliberately left himself hanging. No one would wish to deprive himself of the sheltering truth of the earth like that for the rest of his mortal life.

Shamus —
Raymond Chandler's Philip Marlow —
Shots in the Dark L.A. Style
(Three Novels)

From <u>The Secret of the Golden Flower</u>:

In the purple hall of the City of Jade dwells the God of the utmost emptiness and life.

Philip Marlowe and the L.A. noir. — Private eye — Shamus — Creation of the premier purveyor of hard-boiled detective fiction. — Chandler's Marlowe perceives the city's 1930's surfaces with the keenest of eyes. — As if they reflect everything that is. — Then there is beneath the surface — what's hard and dark and beyond thought or chance of the encroachment of light.

He comes on as a wise guy and somewhat secret agent of decency on his freakish turf. — A boy scout sort of, as well as a practitioner of the time-honored art of running continually afoul of the law.

<u>Golden Flower</u>:

When the one note of individuation enters into birth, human nature and life are divided in two. From this time on, if the utmost quietness is not achieved, human nature and life never see each other again.

Take the liquored up noirish icon Marlowe and the human heart's aspiration to completely chill.... that is, to arrive at itself at some point before or after death.

"Hey man," one wishes to shout at him and Chandler across the decades, "Forget your self-conscious melodrama, your damned old broken hearts of gold, and fashion yourselves into urn-like heaps." — A reflective impersonal ticker surely the best patch for what ails you, what you most truly must be seeking.

C.G. Jung and Marlowe —

In his Record of Two Friendships, Miguel Serrano concludes that the metaphysical novelist, Herman Hesse, achieved greater inner peace than Jung whom he thought of as more of a still aspiring magician. — "Up until the last moment Jung seemed to be searching."

"Shamus" is what they call Marlowe. — A solver of puzzles (crimes), — A magician of sorts as well, searching in his wise guy way for a fix to the pain of living as well as for particular malefactors. Shamus — a private dick to the mysteries of the cosmos. — The deep mysteries that no ordinary shamus would even think of taking on.

Shammes (sexton in a synagogue) is the probable origin of the term according to the American Heritage Dictionary. — Consistent with the broad consensus that there is certain Yiddish cast to the underside of things. That shamus Marlowe, for example, like a lot of men in the process of destroying themselves, didn't scare easily. — There is the circulation of light, the refinement of breath, the beating of the heart and the darkness at the bottom of his bottle of bonded bourbon.

Golden Flower:

The awakening of the spirit is accomplished because the heart has first died. When a man can let his heart die, then the primal spirit wakes to life.

The unreconstructed, only partially knowledgeable hearts of Philip Marlowe and the man who wrote him, floating through a land of opium dreams, cosmetic beauty, perfect weather. Hard liquor rather than the love of countless hot eager babes to comfort, console him.

Marlowe, even down on his uppers, can't be bought, can't be kept, can't even find a bit of respite except with a game of chess that he plays nightly against himself in black and white.

Golden Flower:

Master Lao-Tzu cautions of the hazards and obstacles one faces before reaching the point at which one can sit "like a withered tree before a cliff." Also gives instructions on the correct way of "keeping equal distance between being and non-being."

I remember this last from the days of my misspent youth. — The dull ecstatic choices between those two states that came to the same. — How did we wind up in this decaying metaphysical box? — Could it really be just the passing of the years and the self's defensive amnesia?

Is this Chandler's great theme — mutability in the Hollywood sense? — Fear of death's true play and pleasure?

And if I somehow returned to consistently honest breaths on the ground of being, could I possibly leave everything else behind? Just a fleeting thought before a voice deep inside insists that sucker that I am, I still know the deal.

———————

Marlowe slaps his giggly, coked-up bitches around. Just to sober them up, straighten them out, you understand, although they seem to like it well enough. The predicate is that he's mostly half-drunk himself. Still, a noirish knight in only somewhat tarnished armor.

Shamus / Shammes

Maintaining some kind of order, moral or otherwise, in those L.A. depths. A sense of rectitude one could call it, if one wished to give it a bit of a turn.

Marlowe —

An Ishmael of his private

Underworld

Ironic, uncertain, whistling

Dixie along with the rest of,

Loosely speaking, humanity.

The real and true Shammes at the old Staten Island synagogue at Elizabeth and Delafield. — That kind and pious little man in his white mortality vestments on Yom Kippur. His great respect for my father who reciprocated his respect and friendship and had no use for the bullying rabbi and his mistreatment of his keeper of order.

The shamus Marlowe comes out of a hotel scuffle in <u>The Big Sleep</u> with all the guns in the room stuffed in his pockets. — Can't quite figure out if the heavy and the two dames are so lame or Marlowe that cool. For sure he has an appraising eye for the ladies and the ladies have instant eyes for him. It doesn't come to much. — A vacancy that any student of alcoholic men would understand immediately. Reminding me of old Jew-hating Skip, the manager of a midtown tennis shop where I worked for a few months at the beginning of the seventies. — The ex-minor league first baseman so fucking proud the Nazis hadn't made goddamn soap out of his ass. His stories about escapades with the nurses on some isolated island when he was in the service trailing off to an inevitable "then I got shit-faced" with few variations. — And how can we take Marlowe more seriously except for his literary sensibility?

<u>Golden Flower</u>:

"Furthermore, we must not fall victim to the ensnaring world. The ensnaring world is where the five kinds of demons disport themselves."

Shamus groping through that L.A. labyrinth.

Are the demons really five in number?

Or are they an unholy swarm, crawling all over the walls and ceiling as I remember them? — As Chandler/Marlowe surely experienced them when their hands were played out.

The night both Sternwood sisters in <u>The Big Sleep</u> throw themselves at him in turn, one naked, the other on her way there. After he escapes, he drinks two cups of black coffee, lets us in on the fact that "Women make me sick." — But we sense that phenomenon, the irresistible, private eye. — "Kiss me killer," the older sister Vivian had breathed before he hastily got back to the detecting business. — We wonder about the original wound, before alcohol and whatever other impediments set in.

An awful fear of the dead bang truth / a shattering vision of total loss.

His little moralizing speeches the toughest to take. — Shamus, the woman-hating, woman-fearing Galahad. — There is the big mortal sleep and the booze induced slumber party. — And yet, operatively speaking, there are still moves left on the table....

<u>The Golden Flower</u> admonishes the reader to meditate correctly and thus to enter the space of energy rather than the cave of fantasy. Translator Richard Wilhelm explains some complex meditation

instructions thusly — "The living manner of the circulation of the light has just this meaning: to live mingling with the world and yet in harmony with the light." Most important:

"And the still deeper secret of the secret — the land that is nowhere, that is the true home." — That land as far from Hollywood as could be imagined.

Old lily-white money, long winding driveways leading to big fortress-like homes with heavy wood furniture, discreet butlers and maids, in a paper mache town. Inhabited in The Big Sleep by nearly dead Gen. Sternwood with his decent concern for a disappeared son-in-law; Mr. Grayle, the aging compliant cuckold in Farewell My Lovely; the formidable port swigging Mrs. Murdock in The High Window. — His rich decaying clients and the fast women ancillary to them. He retreats down those winding driveways with retainers against his depression era $25 — per diem, commences to puzzle things out, getting battered by experts in the process. Wanders through the bright L.A. sunshine as if in semi-darkness. The things he holds on to — his morals, professional ethics, bottles of Scotch, have no substance in anything approaching reality. — An almost total eclipse of the true self. Still a certain perverse genius hangs over the proceedings.

In Farewell, Marlowe's self-loathing is narrated with a bit of sardonic misdirection:

"A lovely old woman. I liked being with her. I liked getting her drunk for my own sordid purpose. I was a swell guy. I enjoyed being me. You find almost anything under your hand in my business, but I was beginning to be a little sick to my stomach."

Mrs. Jessie Florian, the frowsy widow in question, gives him a piece of her mind: "Copper smart ... not a real copper at that. Just a cheap shamus." —Neatly summing up our hero's existential situation. — The boozed up streetwise bitch giving it to him good and proper.

———————

Marlowe could make time with rich men's wives lightning quick. — Mrs. Grayle (later unmasked as the long-lost deadly Vilma in <u>Farewell</u>). The usual spectacular blonde, able and more than willing to drink like a fish, tongue like a snake. In the reveal she pumps five slugs into the belly of her ever-loving, neck-snapping Moose Malloy.

<u>The High Window</u> has him nobly rescuing the mousy Miss Merle Davis, with that discreet little automatic in her desk drawer, from her abusive employer, Mrs. Murdock. He manages, somehow, to bundle her off to her neglected, doting mid-western parents on dowager Murdock's dime. — Is the well-meaning private eye really unaware that it's odds-on his putative little Madonna will forever have the highway blues? — She and those other representatives of womankind he is likely to come across in his murky personal and professional practice? Does the secret and inevitable thought of the above seep into his heart and leave him mean, disillusioned and habitually anesthetizing himself with whatever is handy?

———————

As noted, this particular shamus could take a punch, could get off the floor after being "sapped" (sucker-punched), knocked cold with brass knuckles or blind-sided with a fist full of rolled up coins. — Shot full of dope/speed, tied up, tied down, he had a knack for miraculous escapes. Incapable of truckling to money or power, he

didn't seem to know or care what was good for him. Callous and
bigoted with his times as to dirty Jews, Wops, Shines, and never very
far from yielding to the various tendencies toward oblivion that
marked his profession. We'll call him a real sho-nuff American of a
type that's been excised by hypocritical euphemism, true-life
caricatures, current fashion.

Shamefully, in <u>Farewell</u> he flees a nice girl's offer of a much-
needed bed for the night. Fear, it seems, driving him out the door.
Anne Riordan is her dreamy name and an L.A. police lieutenant tips
Marlowe that the auburn-haired sweetheart really digs him.

Says he doesn't like nice girls.

What does he like?

"I like smooth shiny girls, hard boiled and loaded for sin."

Attempting to probe the recesses of Chandler's authorly
imagination, one wonders whether it is love or sex that is the greater
transgressive fear.

As <u>Farewell</u> unspools, we find Marlowe waking up in a
cheap waterfront hotel room staring at the reflection of a red blinking
neon light stretching across the ceiling. A man alone, he steels
himself for what awaits him on the menacing gambling ship
anchored outside Bay City harbor's three-mile limit.

Deadly forces to contend with, and all he's got, proverbially,
is his coat, hat and gun. He feels for the shoulder holstered .38
hanging down to his ribcage, makes sure it's just where he can get at
it in a hurry. — I've been there — a matter of how quickly I could
wrap my hand around the butt of that Smith and Wesson Special,
finger on the trigger and swing it into position for use to deadly effect
if it happened to come to that. On his own, facing erasure around
every corner, behind every door. Yes, how quickly could he get to

that heater with unmitigated clarity?

A given that the cops are on the take or otherwise haltered, that corruption, cowardice, vice the order of the day. Marlowe makes ready to take on the shadowy boss, ready to face death for that piddling per diem and God knows what else.

"The wet air was as cold as the ashes of love."

> A deeply wounded past
> to go with his cynical
> present is the broad hint. —
> Never anything more.

He tells us that he worked as a cop in the D.A.'s office and was fired for insubordination. Now out here in this jittery uncertain space strictly a free agent. — How tough would it have been for him to knuckle under to the opportunists, fools and the ever-shifting pyramid of toadies? — To have shaken hands, smiled, let it slide, signed off on the sickening fraud he knew it all to be? — To not go along with the full understanding that the deck is invincibly stacked against you. — It does take a little something. — That absurd bit of honor that clings to our boozed up, bigoted, heavily damaged shamus. — That I truly hope somehow clung to my wavering self during my decades in the system.

Finally in <u>Farewell</u> as in all these tales, Marlowe independently unravels the intricate mysteries of theft, betrayal and murder most brilliantly and simply.

Leaving only love and death to stand untouched, unfathomable. And the open question as to whether the thread of decency that runs through Chandler's fictions has any living purchase in the here and now.

———————————

Some Perspectives on the Wandering Jew of Life and Legend

Part I –

Wooden statue of Cartaphilus AKA Ahasuerus AKA Isaac Laquidem
AKA...

There's a spare, foot high statue of that legendary Wandering Jew
sitting on a bookshelf at just about eye-level above the writing desk
where I still kill most of my time.

Given to my wife, ever so long ago when she was the young mother of
three, by the well-known Village artist Rifka Angel, a refugee from
Lithuania, who said that it had been a gift to her husband from a
genuine Hawaiian prince.

On that bookshelf for decades now, just north of the
reference work <u>Herman Melville A to Z</u> and a compilation of the Zen
monk Hakuin's brush paintings, <u>The Sound of One Hand</u>.

I examine it closely from the bottom up – the smooth wood
base from which legs above the ankles are embedded to the humble
conical Jew hat pulled down nearly to his eyebrows. My fingertips go
over its surface – I'm guessing some kind of soft stone, cool and
somehow electric to the touch.

It almost falls to the floor as I return it to the shelf, and I take
that as a serious warning. – In the absolute humility of its posture and
mien, it is inviolate. – Don't mess with it. Give its rendering the
respect that age and a mountain of suffering have earned.

The eternal Jew with his pitcher in his right hand near to his waist, left hand balled over his heart. That old hat down near to his eyes, a bit of his nose missing, grave beard and mustache. The impression that the whole face has been subtly abraded by time. There's a folded suggestion of a millennial traveler's robe, a hairline crack bisecting the entire figure at the waist.

The presumably penitent inoffensive wanderer understandably somewhat the worse for wear. Over the years its silence and dignity have attached themselves to my soul so that tonight, newly handled, it seems to suffuse us both in its aura of absurd and improbable courage.

Taking every nick and disfiguration with an imperviousness beyond mere inanimate stoicism. – So it seems to me.

Part II –

Sartre (from <u>Baudelaire</u>):

"But the guilty man has his function in the theocratic universe. He has a right to censure, to punishment and to repentance. He cooperates with the universal order and his misdoing invests him with a religious dignity, a place apart in the hierarchy of beings."

And, by the way, do you know the story of this wandering Jew in Christian legend and lore? — The story of the poor shoemaker Cartaphilus (for that seems to have been the first of the many names he would acquire over a millennium), who was alleged to have struck Jesus and told him to move on as he, bearing his cross, paused for a moment on the way to Golgotha?

Jesus, in his pain and anger was supposed to have told him that he would move, but that Cartaphilus would have to tarry until he returned. And again, according to the legend, the Jew Cartaphilus has been wandering the wide world ever since that moment on the Via Crucis, waiting for the Second Coming and forgiveness of his great sin, followed by release in death from the agony of his cursed existence.

The fatal conflation of the Wandering Jew of legend with the historical Jewish people – his sin of rudeness toward the bearer of the cross with our collective and everlasting guilt. Our pariahhood over two thousand years of homelessness and industrial strength exterminations justified by the Curse. – Everything lined up just so.

In the time it has taken the Romans to raise Jesus on the cross, torment him and leave him for dead, Cartaphilus, in the first of a brilliant series of engravings by Gustave Doré, has aged into the ancient wanderer of the legend – he has assumed his long, white beard, clutches his hat and sad-sack water pitcher to his chest while leaning on a crooked wooden staff. There's a hard slanted rain falling over the illumined ground, and the shoemaker, who didn't grant Jesus a moment's pause, is hurrying out of the holy city of Jerusalem.

In the artist's depiction, he is already beyond the crucified, still breathing Jesus on his right, and his preternaturally old head is inclined in that direction, but not so far as to set his eyes upon him. – Jesus, nailed down and alone, wet and cold as he is dying, stares after his former antagonist, now cursed by him and on the run seemingly forever. Too late for both of them, at least this time around.

A bitter day of affliction it was on which the sky wept for the poor rabbi and his unfortunate brother.

In Brussels

Doré's series of twelve engravings bring the poetry and folklore of
some hundreds of years to life. Taking direct inspiration from a piece
by Pierre Dupont commemorating a purported visit by the Eternal
Jew to Brussels in April 1774, the artist renders him, now going under
the name Ahaseurus, clutching his trademark pitcher and staff, his
enormous white beard trailing after him. He is surrounded by
bemused locals on a hellish dead-end street while three small
children and a gaggle of geese form a more respectfully attentive
outer ring. One little girl in particular clasps her hands in an attitude
of adoration.

Along a stone wall a faceless group of soldiers armed with
pikes is undergoing inspection by their superiors. – It looks to be the
devil himself standing free and clear at the highest point of the
suffocating gothic skyline.

At the Flemish Inn –

The oldest and queerest of all the weird Jews in the great
wide world draws a leering crowd on the steps of a tavern,
underneath a sign for foaming brew. Two stout women hold his
arms to his sides while a third grips his wrists from the front. She
bows down to his waist, just below the tangled tragic beard. – What
knowledge does this comical, but magnetic little Yid possess?

Jesus is a spectral presence above the scene, a cross held
downward in his left hand. A stray dog notices and barks up at him.

In the Middle of a Shipwreck

He sits on top of a jagged rock in a roiling sea, the sky a study
in milky chaos.

The wrecked craft, its sails stripped, sits vertically on a
cliffside, its anchor swinging crazily into the wind. A number of poor

souls appear to be drowning in the merciless sea, but the Wanderer has been damned to a life of suffering without end, or rather to such a life until Jesus returns. As far as the legend is concerned, he is still roaming this hostile earth, still without justification or pardon, but immune from the death for which he is supposed to be fervently praying.

The Black Knight

The Wandering Jew is in search of the Black Knight amidst an apocalyptic army of ghosts deep in the Valley of Death...

The Master of War, of sin and contention, holding the reins of his great horse, sits securely in the saddle. Dismembered bodies, their swords and their pikes, litter the battleground on which that eternally cursed one surveys the nightmare come true. Off to one side some diehard in chain mail is about to let loose an arrow from his crossbow at someone or something.

The Jew seems to grow in stature as he looks about him. He is somehow beyond this tawdry slaughter in which men are set against men for reasons that have nothing to do with themselves.

One senses that the Black Knight dare not show his face in its bloody glory to our poor outcast. – that he will avoid contact at all costs and ride the hell off to further shameful triumphs.

Through the Andes –

His everlasting footsteps take him to the Andes where he is pictured threading his way through a defile surrounded by giant serpents and lizards that fix their baleful attention on him, ready to strike.

This time around he appears to be completely on his own, with no spirit, benevolent or otherwise, to be seen above or below, and for once, even he, inured to the most terrific suffering for the greatest length of time of any man anywhere, looks more than a bit wary. But the wretched fellow is about to step clear, and we can assume that he'll find his way to his next destination.

Thrice cursed in his clairvoyance, he is supposed to be – in contemplation of the event, in the actuality of whatever earthly suffering has been conjured up for him and in the eternal agonized recollection. – The map of the world as a blurred shadow on his furrowed brow.

Fording the Rhine –

Head down now for what feels like forever, he steps carefully over the waves, oblivious to the dark forests and castles of the Rhineland forming a cold backdrop. He clutches his cloak to himself, observes the young boy carrying a cross nearby, the other young spirits of the water sustaining him.

Absorbed in his enigmatic Jew thoughts, he walks on the water with a striking absence of spiritual pride, of any sense of accomplishment at all.

Swiss Valley –

He descends to a Swiss Valley after tramping the Alps, once again just beyond Death's grasp. His great beard parted by the stiffest of winter winds to reveal his battered face.

A snow-white angel burning a fragrant torch hovers over the poor fellow, just below the forbidding icy mountain peaks, as if giving the lie to what is called history and the accumulated wisdom of the ages.

An Old Christian Cemetery –

Perhaps the most terrible of all Doré's depictions of the cursed Jew whose path conjures the historical homelessness of his people.

He emerges in the moonlight traversing yet another valley, this one surrounded by dark cypress trees and sheer mountain cliffs, stumbles on an ancient Christian graveyard with toppled tombstones and upright crosses – sentinels of eternal rebuke.

Are those merely windblown contorted grasses on his right or do we have a vision of the condemned laboring in hell? – For certain the sky above is full of devilish riders carried by terrible nightmare beasts.

Directly in front of him, where he can't miss it, is the damned shadow he casts, crawling with all the death he has witnessed and verily the original cross of our afflictions.

This Jew of ours – of yours and mine, whose restlessness is his sin as well as his punishment...

I dreamed in a dream that started just before sleep that I understood the multiple ambiguities of this figure who the world can't seem to let go of, but now I'm pretty much awake, and the jangled mystery is back. It must be a living fucking nightmare that I'm having – that the wanderer himself endured.

"When did you get here?" the townsman wants to know.

"Yesterday."

"When are you leaving?"

"Tomorrow."

— If he's lucky. If things don't turn ugly overnight.

———————————

Part III –

Herman Melville's <u>Clarel</u>, his epic poem of the Holy Land divided into four sections, the third of which, "Mar Saba," goes right to the matter at hand.

Below the Greek Orthodox monastery of Mar Saba perched
perilously near the edge of a cliff above the gorge of Kedron, a
masque is performed in which the Wandering Jew, again known as
Cartaphilus, is imagined in Jehoshaphat, the biblical Valley of
Judgment, facing the towers of Jerusalem. The actor standing in for
the Jew recites lines that explain that he is eternally drawn back to
the city by their guilty tie to the crucifixion of Jesus. A figure
concealed somewhere among the rocks exposits on "the Jew who
wanders ever" in a perpetually "low state" and then the figure of the
masque, this imagined Cartaphilus, tells the extraordinary story of
his existence as filtered through Melville's empathetic genius.

> "My face begetteth superstition:
> In dungeons of Spain's Inquisition
> Thrice languished I for sorcery,
> An Elymas. In Venice, long
> Immured beneath the wave I lay
> For a conspirator. Some wrong
> On me is heaped, go where I may,
> Among mankind. Hence solitude
> Elect I; in waste places brood
> More lonely than an only god;
>
> ....
>
> Through time so I, Christ's convict grim,
> Deathless and sleepless lurching fare –
> Deathless and sleepless through remorse for Him;
> Deathless, when sleepless were enough to bear."

The immortal sentient martyr. – Man, too much
punishment for too little crime as they say in America's ghetto jails.
And the terrible loneliness of the thousand streets punctuated by the
classic interrogation.

> — When did you say you got here?
>
> And how quickly can you pack yourself up?
>
> — Tomorrow early, at the latest.

The weariest of all weary blues.

———————

I visited Mar Saba a little more than a decade ago. Still barely accessible by narrow winding road. In the incensed semi-darkness of the church itself, the walls are lined with glass cases full of the skulls of martyrs bashed by Arab tribesmen from the very early years of the Christian centuries. Before the creation of the monastery, men living in shallow caves within the cliffs atop of which Melville could have witnessed a performance of some sort out of which he may have fashioned his timeless masque. Men ready to die in search of a higher experience of an unknowable kind.

A black-clad monk looking and acting like he stepped out of Kazanzakas's <u>Zorba</u>, shoves a pair of ill-fitting pants in my hands, insists I cover my bare legs before entering the sacred precincts. The women in our group – Melville scholars and wives thereof are denied entry, grouped under a bare tree in the sizzling midday heat of June in the highlands of Israel. – Must have been two hours with no relief of any kind.

Melville's most striking mid-19th century impression:

The barrenness of Judea.

Raymond Weaver, his first biographer, calls it the predominant note in <u>Clarel</u>.

The stony barrenness and humiliation of the land and the refugee people that he found, leading him to thoughts of the Cursed One in the prophet Joel's Valley of Judgment.

Part IV – Opa-locka –

     "I am the end product...of an infinitude of disasters, a multitude of humiliations. In some deep way my sanity consists of loyalty to these misfortunes."
                 — Ben Hecht, "Shylock My Brother"

     Walking down that old Dixie Highway of real and authentic memory – my perplexity and dispossession transparent to the young cracker riding the back of a battered pickup truck. – He clocked me immediately as I stumbled along the side of the road. "Jew," he noted out loud, as much to himself as to me.

     There's a particularized enunciation of the "J" in Jew that's a distinguishing feature of southern speech, and that young man got all of it. – More than sixty years down the line I can still hear its echo, am still grateful for its bracing clarification.

     My father and I had been driving those shimmering hallucinatory south Florida roads for some months in an off-white

Ford Fairlane purchased with sleight of hand credit and now on the very brink of being repossessed, with a leaking radiator that we didn't have the money to properly repair. Barely able to scrape together the change for the cheap fix liquids and powders we poured into the mouth of the radiator to keep the leak in check. The thing just sizzling when the cap was removed that Florida summer of 1959. Very frequent stops for gas and water to cool it down. My old man so broke he was buying gas a dollar a pop. – Never enough cash to really gas up even if the radiator wasn't fit to explode. So broke he couldn't bring himself to part with more than a buck at a time even though that meant we were always in danger of running out of gas somewhere or other and did so on several occasions. And the poor man, terribly down on his luck, with only his dumbass young son as a companion in that awful season of our lives, once agonized aloud when we had stalled somewhere and one of us would have to walk however far it was to the next gas pump to fill the can we kept in the trunk of the car, "Why do I do that?" – And I don't think looking back he didn't know he couldn't bring himself to cough up more cash when we were down to almost none and riding on empty stomachs in the bargain. But I believe I muttered something to the effect that he couldn't help himself before we moved on.

All that time he was looking for some kind of angle, some kind of deal to get us on our feet. – What we both feverishly thought of as a way out.

The chain of bankruptcies, misjudgments, lapses of all sorts, history for another day. – No money for groceries back home in Miami except by kiting checks at the local supermarkets, and every damned check generating a felony warrant under state law. For sure we had to think of something pretty quick ...

Somehow something did come up. Leo, an old union pal
from the Teamster wars in New York, who remembered him from
before he and things had gone so wrong, was ready to put up real
cash for a stake in the right gas station in the right location, betting on
the man he had once known, rather than the desperate fellow with a
rap sheet beside me. And here we were, headed for Opa-locka where
such a prosperous station was advertised for sale.

A Cities Service Center, green with neat, white trim – I forget
the documented gallons per month pumped, but it was a substantial
number, supplemented by kerosene sales in what they called winter.
An honest living is what it shaped up as, and a living is what he had
been desperately searching for. – No more grandiose plans to get
filthy rich and dwell like a potentate. That stuff had been shattered
for now. A living. Shelter for my mother and kid sister and release
from this netherworld for me.

A living. After the bust up of his trucking business in New
York and a nearly deadly turn with aggrieved shylocks and the
disintegration of his big deal real estate plans down here. A phone
call to Leo who gave the go ahead. Okay with the proprietor as long
as we came up with the cash required. – Just had to run it by the
regional Cities Service manager who drove over and had a little
conversation with my old man just out of earshot. A very nice, clean
cut, youngish American wearing a fresh white short-sleeved shirt
with a ballpoint pen clipped to the front pocket, and we're not going
to call him a bigot. No, I still don't think so. Just not sure how the
people down there would handle a Jew-owned station is what it came
down to, and who could blame him?

When I came back to the Fairlane after a visit to the
washroom, I found my father behind the wheel, tears silently

streaming down his cheeks. Remembering back, I believe that dumb as I was, I knew better than to say a word. As noiselessly as possible, I got into the front seat next to him, looking straight ahead. He turned the key in the ignition, and we were on our way to wherever the past and the future were to take us.

Yeah, I think I'm what's called an old man now and the memories of that particular desperate episode are getting a bit dimmer, but I'm quite sure that we were reminded (in a gentlemanly way) down in Opa-locka of who we were and how things are. – How could we have forgotten?

I mean, who were we kidding? And the answer, as it came to me with the tears still rolling down his cheeks as we moved on, was only ourselves. No one else but ourselves.

Shenkin Street

A broken-down old Jew played a slow blues in the midday sun
on Shenkin Street in Tel Aviv, filling the air,
pervading all & everything – El & Elohim & Adonai –
the whole universe & all that which is within it.
        And I wondered how he got there,
The path that he took
to that particular spot
known in the guidebooks for its restaurants
& smart shopping
    as I dropped a handful of shekels into his guitar case.
        We nodded to each other, no longer quite strangers
after 2000 years, now that there was a blues
beyond annihilation between us.
        Beyond humiliation, the denial of our existence
& the crouching enemy at the gate;
        Beyond the good hearts all around that need
must deny themselves.
        With the real & true blues, you know,
it's a matter of feeling everything's going to be all right.

───────────────

Aspects of these very same blues
float over the Judean hills
        to the Mount of Temptation
overlooking the River Jordan as it flows into the Dead Sea;

Float to the Wailing Wall where I remembered
the suffering of my father & grandfathers
& what it means to be a Jew before & then
after we stop kidding ourselves.

        With the weight of history on my shoulders,
It was cool to the touch of my forehead
& fingertips.
Not just a pile of Roman fortress stones to me
& even if they are,
it still exists,
        I still exist,
Our blues are our blues & exist.

———————————

        Fresh from the memory of Jerusalem
& the narrow lane through the Damascus Gate
with feral cats everywhere, a testament to
the feelings of the people for the helpless
living things among them.
These blues are dangerously close to unlocking
my closed old heart in this very moment;
dangerously close to taking me into the
empty unclaimed space in which resides
the truth.
On Shenkin Street, the blues wafting over me, I was wandering no
more.
        God Almighty,
                by whatever name or silence
you choose to be known,

how is it that there is not a place on

this earth for everyone?

    By what law of being must we give up

our humanity?

    How dare they?

Think of the hot little mommas on the streets

& beaches of Tel Aviv, cute as can be,

with the reckless courage of their lives.

    There is the truth of being beyond words,

the stars up above

& the freshly rained on streets

  down below.

    Get ready to meet your maker

if you can find Him

  I tell myself,

  The low dark clouds moving slowly north

over New York City

after the shrouded sun has mysteriously arisen

www.ingramcontent.com/pod-product-compliance
Lightning Source LLC
Chambersburg PA
CBHW060521030426
42337CB00015B/1964